I0599397

# The New Hermetics Equinox Journal

## Volume Three

# The New Hermetics Equinox Journal

## Volume Three

Sun in Aries 0° 0′ 0″ March 2009 C.E.

Edited by Jason Augustus Newcomb

New Hermetics Press
Sarasota, FL

First published in 2009 by
The New Hermetics Press
P. O. Box 18111
Sarasota, FL 34276
www.newhermetics.com

ISBN: 978-0-578-02326-7


Cover Design and typesetting by Fr∴ E. I. A. E.


16 15 14 13 12 11 10 09
8 7 6 5 4 3 2 1

*kite on a warm breeze*
*just one thread keeping it here--*
*her hands don't let go*

# Contents

# Editorial Introduction

By Jason Augustus Newcomb

At last! The third volume of this new series devoted to the continued expansion and evolution of the New Hermetics is here. As always, I am very excited about this latest volume. This series is finally hitting its stride, and I am thrilled that so many diverse ideas and opinions are finally being expressed. Subjects as diverse as Enochian Magick, Candle Magick, Talismans, General Semantics and Śaivist Tantra are discussed in these pages and I am really pleased.

Once again this book begins with an article that is quite silly. It is probably the silliest so far, but I will strive for even greater silliness in upcoming volumes. Enjoy!

In future volumes I would love to receive even more essays from the people who are working with these tools around the world. What I would ideally like to publish in these volumes is the real experiences of people working with these tools, both people's anecdotes and idiosyncratic modifications of these tools. Every magician is a unique microcosm, and it may be that your insights provide a better vehicle for another's evolution than my own. I also welcome submissions of poetry, stories, or black and white artwork inspired by the New Hermetics or really any metaphysical trip you care to share. The ideal method of submission would be digitally on a CD, sent to:

The New Hermetics Press
Journal Submissions
P.O. Box 18111
Sarasota, FL 34276

This journal is published biannually. The submission deadlines are:

Autumnal Equinox Volume: July 15th

Spring Equinox Volume: January 15th

At this time there is no financial compensation for publication in the journal as its circulation is fairly small and the costs of printing high. But the contributors of any articles or artwork printed in this series will retain the copyright on their works and will always be completely free to publish them elsewhere as long as any contract signed elsewhere does not restrict their continued inclusion in these volumes.

Jason Augustus Newcomb
March 20th, 2009

# Oracles for the
# New Hermetics
# at the
# Vernal Equinox

## From the Tarot

The High Priestess

## From the I Ching

Hexagram 18 changing to Hexagram 2

## From Liber AL

III, 38

## The Word of the Equinox

SMARANANDA

# The Great Occult Question
By Jason Augustus Newcomb

Since time immemorial, serious inquirers into the field of occultism have asked one question more than any other. This profound question has boggled the minds of some of our brightest luminaries, and bewildered many of our most astute historical scholars. This question, left unanswered, threatens to crack the very foundations of the magical edifice. It is such an obvious question hanging above all gatherings of occultists that I almost feel it unnecessary to articulate. But I will do so, nonetheless. The great question is: Why is it that occultists are so darn fat? In this article I hope to finally lay out a clear and simple answer to this tremendously heavy question once and for all.

Certainly, it isn't fair to say that *all* occultists are fat. There are some occultists that are quite skinny. Some are even rather athletic. But it does seem that most of the *greatest* occultists are heavyweights. In fact, if you were to attend a pagan festival, an esoteric conclave housed in one of our nation's finer hotel conference halls, a local magical book store, or a magical community center, in short, anyplace that occultists gather for the exchange of ideas and good cheer, you could try an experiment. If you looked about the room and noted the very fattest people, the most bloated and round, the fattest of the fatties, without a doubt those people would eventually hoist their girth up to the podium and lecture on all matters arcane, spiritual, and often quite confusing.

But why is it that great occultists are so fat? Some might say that it is unfair to make this speculation at all because in modern times so many in the general populace are fat. Perhaps it is not that great occultists are fat, but simply that we are living in an age of fatties. However, if we look back through history we can see that occultists have always been a fat lot. Looking back a few generations, we need only cast our glance on Aleister Crowley and his contemporaries in the Golden Dawn, and we see a group of chubby metaphysicists filling their gullets with plover's eggs and brandy. Many of the photographs that we have of Mr. Crowley display that ample belly which loved to be filled with all manner of exotic, and fattening, delicacies from around the world. William Wynn Westcott and George Cecil Jones of the Golden Dawn both shared Crowley's tubby phys-ique. Their contemporary Helena Petrovna Blavatsky never turned down a rack of pork ribs in her life. Going back a bit further into the nineteenth century, we find the plump Eliphas Levi waddling heavily around his circle as he conjured the chunky shade of the corpulent Appolonius of Tyana. From Henry Cornelius "Bacon Butt" Agrippa, Edward "Wide Load" Kelly, to Theo-phrastus Bombastus "Thunder Thighs" Paracelsus we can easily discern that the great occultists are nearly always fat. Plato, Aristotle, Socrates, these were all hefty heifers. The Buddha, though sometimes depicted in the skinny façade of his ascetic youth, was nonetheless quite a rotund enlightened being once he realized that simple starvation did not equal enlightenment. He was a big fat man, as were many of his students and boddhisattvas, big sausage-eating fellows. Although, I guess they were probably vegetarians or something. At least so they claimed. Who knows what goes on during those secret Tantric rites? They certainly got pretty chunky somehow.

In many cases the fatness of an occultist can be the measure of their greatness. For instance, I am a rather fat occultist, and I am certainly a great occultist. It is in part by my fatness that you can know that I am a great occultist. However, in comparison with a great hefty adept like Lon Milo Duquette, I am practically svelte. And Lon is certainly a greater occult luminary than I am. The superior girth of Lon Milo Duquette is in direct proportion to his superiority over me as an occult superstar.

The speculation on why these great occultists are so fat has taken many turns. There are many different theories that have been put forth. Some have suggested that it is because of the greatness of their knowledge and the greatness of their minds. The idea is that such a wealth and even surplus of great knowledge could only be contained by a larger than life body. While this is certainly a clever and understandable speculation, it doesn't take into account great men like Gandhi or even Jesus who were quite lithe and slender in their physique and yet must be counted amongst the more knowledgeable of humankind's progeny. So we cannot for certain assert this as an explanation for the fatness of the great occultists.

Some theorists have asserted that the great occultists are fat simply because they have eaten many of the lesser occultists to gain their power and wisdom. There may be something to this, but I dare not say more.

Another theory that has been put forth in the field of earnest inquiry into explaining the fat occultist pheno-menon is that the great occultists are suffering from bad karma. The wealth of knowledge that they possess has been hard won through countless past in-carnations, and all manner of karmic debt has been acquired over millennia spent in the ruthless pursuit of dark and secret power and arcane truths. This theory purports that great occultists are so fat because by being so very big, they can process and release a big amount of karma, and thus become free from the endless cycle of rebirth that much more quickly. While the ratio of fat to karma has yet to be scientifically or statistically calculated, there is certainly some possibility that a relationship may one day be discovered. But because this theory is so incredi-bly silly, barely making any sense at all, we are forced to place it merely in the 'maybe' category. Thinking about it, it doesn't really make any sense at all. I don't know why I even mentioned it.

However, as a card carrying member of the fraternity of big fat occultists, I would like to finally reveal the true reason for our fatness. Though it may cost me my seat at the fried chicken council, and even my leadership position in the fudge subcommittee, I feel it is only fair to finally give you the truth. The reason that occultists are so darn fat is probably simply because they really, really, really love sugar and cheese. Sometimes the simplest explanation is the only one necessary, even for occultists. Thank you and goodnight.

# Operationalism in Occult Work
## By Frater Eheieh Ahabah

So you believe you want to be a Magician. When you found the New Hermetics, you may have thought that you finally found a workable, useful system that would bring you to realize that desire. Those who choose to work in a supervised program may even find that they believe their supervising Adept will help them in their path to become a Magician.

When we engage the tools of The New Hermetics - or any system of Magick - we willfully initiate the processes of self-transformation. We learn the primacy of clearly formulating goals. We methodically apply particular techniques toward attaining those goals. Finally, we close the loop by evaluating our effectiveness at bringing about a particular transformation in our sphere of experience... our own particular 'reality-tunnel'.

When I initially started working through The New Hermetics, I found myself quite focused on learning to clearly define goals and practicing particular methods and techniques. I did not give much thought to my evaluational methods. As I grew interested in studying some of the background material that The New Hermetics draws from (in particular the works of Robert Anton Wilson, Israel Regardie, Richard Bandler & John Grinder), I started to notice frequent mentions of 'General Semantics' and its developer, Alfred Korzybski. The discipline of General Semantics deals with evaluating our evaluations. As simple as this may sound, I believe it has significant implications that bring us to the foundation of Magick: willed self-transformation.

Each of us creates models by which we operate day-to-day within our particular 'reality-tunnel'. For example, as you scan these structured blots of ink on this page with your optical receptors some of the photons emanating from an energy source (perhaps a light fixture attached to the ceiling of a room you currently occupy) reflect off the structure of the page with its ink blots and interact with the structure of your optical receptors. The kinetic energy that results from these transactions creates microscopic structural changes along the nerves attaching your optical receptors to your larger brain structure. Your functioning nervous system - particularly the brain - then creates a representation of those events by abstracting information from this closed-feedback loop (think of pressing on one area of a ketchup packet and observing the movement elsewhere). You 'see' the abstraction of the events rather than the events themselves. In short, you see a model.

We further use this process of abstracting when we apply labels to those models. We evaluate the model against our experiences and determine an appropriate symbol to represent the model. We use these symbols to communicate information about the model, both internally and externally. This describes the function and structure of language. Due to the self-reflexive nature of language, we can further label our labels... symbolize our symbols. Some labels only describe other labels rather than describing a model. General Semantics promotes an awareness of the process of abstraction. By operating with this consciousness of abstraction, we can learn evaluate more effectively.

Each particular operational model contains certain assumptions. When we make evaluations (come to conclusions), we operate under these assumptions. Adequate assumptions tend toward useful conclusions. Inadequate assumptions tend to faulty conclusions. Also, the assumptions in one model may not necessarily reflect those of another. Each model operates with a relatively independent set of assumptions.

When we lose our 'awareness of abstraction' (easy until this awareness becomes second nature), we begin to identify with a particular model and accept its implicit assumptions without question. An operating model thus becomes an identity...an ego projection. The structure of one's models, one's 'egos', gives rise to the nature of one's 'reality-tunnel'.

Identifying with a particular role (spouse, employee, friend, writer, teacher, magician, etc.), these assumptions translate to expectations. As long as we have our expectations met, all seems well in our particular 'reality-tunnel'. When we find our expectations not met, we find ourselves feeling disappointment, anger, frustration, etc. When we identify with a particular role, it would seem that our equilibrium depends on having the particular expectations we associate with that role met. This describes the essence of the fear/desire duality found described in various traditions.

At this point, you may find yourself wondering how we can apply these ideas in a practical way. To illustrate, consider goal setting in the context of the New Hermetics. We can use these principles when formulating our goals in a way that empowers us to attain the transformations we seek. Compare the following sets of goals:

| | |
|---|---|
| I will be a musician. | I will write and perform music. |
| I will be an author. | I will write and publish a series of short stories. |
| I will be a painter. | I will express my creativity by painting a canvas. |
| I will be generous. | I will do something that I find generous. |

The first sets of goals, each beginning with "I will be..."represent a projection of identity. They focus on 'being' (and 'not being') something. The second set of goals focus on doing something specific and measurable. We do not find the dogma associated with the expectations of egos 'being' one thing and 'not being' something else. Consequently, evaluating the effectiveness of our transformations becomes much more reliable. We more easily find what works to bring us closer to our goals (and thus more empowerment) and where we may need to adjust.

The usefulness of this orientation extends beyond goal setting. When working with our values and beliefs, we would do well to pay particular attention to how many of our values and beliefs center around ideas of "being" something-or-other. When changing our values or beliefs from "being" one thing to "being" something else, we still find ourselves the bonds of ego attachment and no closer to attaining a meaningful spiritual breakthrough.

Do you want to 'be' a Magician, or do you want to 'do' (practice, work, etc.) Magick? If you can differentiate between the two, then you will find this particular evaluational orientation quite easy and natural. If you still find yourself stuck in the particular orientation that does not differentiate between 'being' something and 'doing' something, do not despair. You already have the tools necessary to reorient (transform) yourself, and you will find yourself surprised at how much easier your Magick seems when evaluating in terms of 'doing' rather than 'being'.

# Vijñänabhairava
## A New English Translation
By Jason Augustus Newcomb

For a long time I've treasured the little Tantric text *Vijñänabhairava*. For me it is one of the most interesting religious documents I've ever read. It has helped me immensely in studying Tantra, Magick, and enlightenment in general. What I find so interesting about it is that it contains both a large number of practical methods for obtaining enlightened awareness, but also in its brief way contains a philosophical outlook that I find very refreshing and fascinating. It expresses the essence of Tantra in a way that no other text, ancient or modern, has ever achieved. It focuses on taking all potential experiences in life and turning them into vehicles for discovering the enlightened awareness that is always there in the background.

I possess six separate translations of the text, but none of them fully satisfy me. Some of the translations are far too free, frequently misrepresenting the original intention of the tantra. Others lean so heavily toward a technical discussion of the philosophy of Kashmir Shaivism that the simplicity of the text is lost in a sea of jargon. It is really an invisible translation, combining the best in each of the other translations, that really is most meaningful to me. This invisible text has had a profound background influence on my life and my work. I thought it only fair to share it with this community. So here I will attempt to render my invisible translation into a readable and visible form.

I first discovered the *Vijñānabhairava* many years ago when I read *Zen Flesh Zen Bones* by Paul Reps. A version of this text forms the fourth section *of Zen Flesh Zen Bones* where it is misnamed or else strangely spelled *Vijyana Bhairava*.[1] The text in *Zen Flesh Zen Bones* is not really a translation of the text of the *Vijñānabhairava*. Rather it is a very free poeticizing of most of the text, likely without access to the original at all. It is quite a lovely little piece however, it really moved me when I read it in my teens, and continues to stir that silent uplifted place to this day.

With mystifying phrases like "Unminding mind, keep in the middle- until" the *Vijyana Bhairava* in *Zen Flesh Zen Bones* manages to capture the essence of both Tantra and Zen in a succinct and rather melodious way. But this is not at all an accurate portrayal of the original Sanskrit. The above śloka is somewhat better rendered in my "Dissolve consciousness of the body everywhere into the crown with firm one-pointed practice and the essence of the goal will be revealed." Still, I'm sure you

---

[1] It was rather amusing to discover that Bhagwan Shree Rajneesh (AKA "Osho") based his "tantric" manual *The Book of Secrets* entirely upon this text found in *Zen Flesh Zen Bones.* He treats this rather inaccurate translation as gospel with frequently absurd results. Here an Indian teacher is basing his enlightened discourse on a very faulty American translation of an Indian text. It clearly shows what an interesting rascal Rajneesh really was. You would find this fact particularly amusing if you could see how pedantic Rajneesh gets about the details of the text when those details were so divergent from the Sanskrit original. There's a laugh on every page. Nonetheless, Rajneesh did have some interesting ideas that are worth exploring - with a mountain of salt.

can see the simple beauty of the former phrase. Today there are many English translations of the original Sanskrit text of *Vijñānabhairava*, but they are largely a bit too technical and stilted. For instance, the translation of Jaideva Singh reads, "When the body of the yogi is penetrated by consciousness in all parts of his mind which has become firm by one-pointedness (drdhibhutam) is dissolved in the dvadasanta situated in the body, then that yogi whose intellect has become firm experiences the characteristic of Reality."

With this present translation I hope to capture something of the flowing beauty I discovered many years ago in *Zen Flesh Zen Bones*, while somewhat more accurately representing the text itself. I'm not the first to attempt this as *Vijñānabhairava* is a very popular text in Tantric circles. Hopefully my attempt will add something to these efforts.

*Vijñānabhairava* was written or "received" sometime between 700-1000 C.E. It teaches one hundred and twelve different meditation practices or "dharanas" that are all designed to center consciousness on our own divinity, our "Bhairava" or "Śiva" consciousness. The majority of the *Vijñānabhairava* is taken up with this rather long catalogue of different meditative practices, all intended to lead you toward non-dual awareness. The instructions are not terribly detailed, although most of them are simple enough that no more instruction is really necessary to put them into use.

The key to all these practices is to engage them with one-pointed concentration, silencing your mind completely. Although one hundred and twelve practices are described, there is really only one practice. That practice is integrating all aspects of consciousness and experience into unity in this present moment.[2] This text is a fairly advanced one. It will be most useful to adepts that are seeking an understanding of the non-dual state. This is not everyone's cup of tea. Some people are quite happy dwelling in a dualistic universe and I do not mean to imply, by my inclusion of this text here, that the ultimate goal of the New Hermetics is the radical non-dual philosophy or practice of Kashmir Shaivism. I find this little book useful in my own work, and I like to share things. But you do not have to accept this philosophy to enjoy this little Tantric text.

What I find so interesting about this text is that although the purpose is quite simple: non-dual awareness, the sheer number of strategies proposed as possible techniques for obtaining this state is staggering. Practices from variations on breath awareness, mantra recitation to sexual copulation are all proposed as possible vehicles. Even unusual practices such as contemplating the empty space within a jar, focusing on extreme states such as anger or fear, sneezing, or even rubbing your eyes and concentrating on the sparks of light that appear are suggested as methods that can lead to enlightenment. Every aspect of life, eating, sleeping, love-making, breathing, walking, dancing, swaying and everything in between can be turned into a vehicle for connecting more deeply with the divine in everything. Virtually every conceivable aspect of life, both inner and outer, can be a vehicle for realization, and most if not all of these potential vehicles are listed concisely and practically in the following pages.

Wherever possible I have removed strictly technical Sanskrit terms, replacing them with more universally understandable language. In some cases this has not

---

[2] In this, the *Vijñānabhairava* agrees rather wholeheartedly with the recent writings of Eckhart Tolle and other popular non-dual writers.

been possible so I've tried to offer explanatory notes where really necessary. Nonetheless, I have attempted to remain as true as possible to the meaning in the original text. Other translations have been much more interested in either expressing the idiosyncratic spiritual agendas of the translators, or else displaying the translator's great understanding of the technical jargon and metaphysics of Śaivism. I think the simple message of the text stands well enough on its own. In a future book I may offer a more detailed commentary, but for now I think the text itself will suffice. Words such as "chakra" or "mantra" that have entered into common parlance in our language have generally been left in Sanskrit.

I should add that I am a mystic and magician, not a scholar of Sanskrit. My knowledge of the language confines itself mostly to the mystical jargon that I have acquired through studying Indian religious texts translated into English. I would never attempt to translate something like this without English references. Because of this I have carefully compared my translation with the six others at my disposal and I hope I haven't made too many grievous errors. I am also not an expert scholar of Kashmir Śaivism, although I have read a considerable amount of the extant literature on the subject. I can only hope that my translation does not garble any of the difficult esoteric concepts of Śaivism too badly.

There is a lot of coded communication in this text as in all tantric texts. I have attempted to make this "twilight language" as clear as I can, but this is not always possible when there are multiple layers of meaning that are clearer in Sanskrit than in English. In general, some of the dharanas are easier to understand than others. A few are so obscure that they may not be useful at all to you. Others are easily recognizable from other spiritual

systems, or are even quite similar to some of the New
Hermetics practices.

I don't want to delve too deeply here into the religion
or esoteric philosophy of Śaivism. My presentation of
this text is because I find it very interesting, inspiring
and instructive. I am in no way attempting to convert
anyone to any religion. The text itself is a mystical
instruction for obtaining experiences in consciousness,
not a religious text at all per se. But in order to
understand it fully I will explain a few concepts in case
you are unaware of them. First and foremost let me
discuss the dramatis personae of the text. As with most
tantric texts, the *Vijñānabhairava* consists of a dialogue
between the male and female aspects of ultimate divinity. They are the ultimate as god and goddess, twin
halves of our own highest consciousness. Although they
are in actuality an indivisible unity, for the sake of the
text they converse. In this sort of text, one member of the
pair operates as the teacher and the other as the student.
In this text the male half represents the teacher and the
female the student. In some tantras this relationship is
the other way around, but in our text the male half of the
divine pair acts as teacher. The male god is called called
Bhairava, but also Śiva or Deva in the text, and these
terms are more or less synonymous. Bhairava is an
epithet of Śiva. If you are familiar with tantric Tibetan
Buddhism then you may have come across the name
"Bhairava" as one of the deities that the tantric god-
forms of the Chakrasamvara tradition tread upon. In
fact, Bhairava is quite similar in aspect to Chakrasamvara because part of the latter's tradition is that he
conquered Bhairava and took on his appearance. At any
rate, images of Bhairava represent him as a "wrathful"

form of Śiva with a dark and scowling beastly visage.[3] Bhairava is a dark, terrible and frightening god-form often depicted with long, sharp teeth, weapons and severed human heads as ornaments. This kind of iconography is fairly common in Tantric art. On the other hand, sometimes Bhairava is represented as a beautific yogi, or even a skeletal creature. The text however explains that this is all merely "a magical deception" and that Bhairava is a state of consciousness, the highest state of non-dual awareness. Śiva too is this highest consciousness, the true non-dual Self. There may be a subtle distinction intended between the terms, with Śiva representing a more lofty stage of the process, but this is not important for a simple and practical under-standing of the text. The two terms can basically be seen as interchangeably representative of the highest state of non-dual divine consciousness.

The same can be said for the other half of the dia-loguing pair who is referred to variously as Śri Devi, Bhairavi, Śakti, and terms of endearment such as blessed one or gazelle-eyed one. Although Bhairava is ostensibly teaching her, he frequently discusses her own role in the process of obtaining enlightenment in the third person. Don't allow this to confuse you. His "teaching" of her is only a literary device so that he can teach you. "Śakti" as a more technical term also occurs frequently in the text within the dharanas themselves where it takes on ano-ther shade of meaning. Śakti basically means "power." In tantric philosophy, the male Śiva exists in a reposed transcendental void, and when active, as in creating or destroying the universe, it is his female half, his Śakti or power that is actively working. There are numerous divisions in Śakti, or many Śaktis, with different kinds of

---

[3] In many ways Bhairava is quite similar to Aleister Crowley's metaphysical conception of the god Pan.

power in different levels of subtlety. These nuances are not essential to working with the text at hand. I should however mention that the specific Śaktis mentioned are generally pranaśakti or kundaliniśakti. But they are after all ultimately one Śakti, and joined completely in unity with Śiva. Understanding this will hopefully help you make better sense of this term in context.

Kashmir Śaivism takes a completely non-dual view of the universe. The entire universe is Śiva. Every object or particle is Śiva. It is not that the sum total of the separate chunks of the universe becomes Śiva when added together. Each little piece is the entirety of Śiva. The book you are holding is Śiva, each letter on each page is Śiva, each molecule, each galaxy, each chunk of whatever size is Śiva in his entirety. Every experience is Śiva perceiving Śiva, or to perhaps put it more accurately, every experience is simply Śiva. The perception of two Śivas or even hundreds of billions of billions of Śivas is the basic stumbling block that has us believing that we are all separate and enslaved. But the enslavement is entirely self-created and easily dropped. It is all but the expansion and contraction, the joyful dance, of Śiva. Breaking perception down into its most basic elements there are really only two experiences in consciousness: the experience of "I" and the experience of "other." When these two collapse into one that is enlightenment. The way the text proposes we do this is to silence the mind using one or more of a hundred and twelve different approaches.

In this text you will find many "verifications" of some of the premises of "new thought" type movements like those outlined in popular books such as *The Secret*. However, here these ideas are taken to their more logical conclusion. Yes, I am ultimately one with the universe. And there is absolutely nothing "wrong" with pleasure, affluence or personal gain. But that doesn't necessarily mean I should use my infinite consciousness to manifest a fancy new car for my little self, or get my bills paid by mysterious checks from the aethyr. It means that I don't have to play such games any more at all. Whether my tiny, personal body exists in poverty or wealth is irrelevant to my infinity. Pursuing game pieces will just tend to pull me away from my cosmic wonder. That is, unless I can somehow do so without caring about the result. But it is certainly not forbidden or evil to experience sensory pleasures, and I can pursue them if I wish to, knowing that such things are ultimately meaningless and useless.[4]

The text of *Vijnanabhairava* consists of one hundred and sixty three ślokas, or couplets of Sanskrit verse. The first twenty-three are in the form of a question and answer session between Bhairava and Bhairavi, or Śiva and Śakti, describing what Bhairava is and is not. This section was only given a marginal inclusion in *Vijyana Bhairava*. Ślokas ten through thirteen are particularly interesting in that they clearly propose that all outward religious forms, rituals and customs are just "candy for babies." Ślokas twenty four through one hundred and thirty seven consist of the one hundred and twelve dharanas. It is sometimes a bit difficult to tell when one dharana ends and another begins. Depending on how you divide them up you could see them as considerably fewer or more than one hundred and twelve dharanas. But the text itself mentions that there are one hundred and twelve. Tradition has divided them into the "one hundred and twelve" in a few different ways. Again, I will simply let the text stand on its own. The remaining ślokas after the dharanas offer the stunning conclusion that will only make sense if you carefully read the text

---

[4] Do what thou wilt shall be the whole of the Law.

from beginning to end. This conclusion is entirely absent from the text in *Zen Flesh Zen Bones.*

# Vijñänabhairava

## The Gnosis of Supreme Awakening

# Vijñānabhairava

1.  Śrī Devi said: Oh Deva I have already heard the entirety of the great philosophies and scriptures of Śaivism.

2.  But even now my doubts are not fully removed. What in reality is the essential nature of Bhairava? Are you the creative energy contained in the collection of sacred letter sounds?

3.  Does your reality consist of the nine different forms of Bhairava as in the Bhairava tradition? Or the three-headed God? Or is it in the three kinds of Śaktis?

4.  Is your essential nature in the power of mantra present in all words (nada)? Or is it in the power of mantra present in every object in the universe (bindu)? Or the subtler and subtler sounds? Is it some mysterious power ascending in the chakras? Does it reside in the vowel-less sound of 'ha?' Or is it the form of Śakti?

5.  Are you both transcendent and immanent or are you wholly transcendent or wholly immanent? If you are wholly transcendent then this transcendence is contradictory.

6.  The transcendent cannot be divided into separate forms or colorful bodies. The transcendent is indivisible and cannot be made of composite parts.

7.    Oh Lord, please grace me by completely remov-
      ing my doubts. Bhairava answered: Very good
      questions! They are the essence of the Tantras, oh
      dear one.

8.    Noble lady, this is the most secret teaching, but I
      will reveal it to you. This composite form of
      Bhairava that you mention is a magical deception.
      It has no essence.

9.    It is just an illusion, like a delusional city in the
      sky.

10.   The descriptions of the form of Bhairava are only
      given as a meditation for people who have con-
      fused minds, for those who delight in osten-
      tatious rituals and empty external practices, for
      those who are stuck in dualistic thinking. These
      practices help guide them toward the real con-
      templation.

11.   In reality, I do not have nine forms, nor am I
      within the multitude of letter sounds. I am not a
      three-headed God and I am not the essence of the
      three Śaktis.

12.   I am neither in nada nor bindu, nor any subtle
      sound, nor in the piercing of the chakras, and my
      essence is not even to be found in Śakti.

13.   All these descriptions are like frightening tales to
      discipline unruly children or sweets given by a
      mother to bribe them into obedience. They are
      meant only for immature minds, to help them
      behave ethically (until they are ready for the final

realization that Bhairava is their own essential Self).

14.   The true state of consciousness known as Bhairava is blissfully free from all limitations of space, time and form. It is entirely inexpressible and indescribable.

15.   It can only be known in the bliss of your own inner experience, free from dichotomizing thought patterns, beyond all thought. This state of unity consciousness is alone the Śakti of Bhairava who is known as Bhairavi and utterly one with me.

16.   This is the true nature of my essential self, united without dualities in all-inclusive fullness. In this supreme reality, how can there be any object of worship? Who could be the worshipper? Who is there to be worshipped?

17.   The supreme Goddess is the transcendental form of the Bhairava consciousness which exists so that it can be described.

18.   Since Śakti and her Lord are identically one, as there is no difference between a quality and the possessor of the quality, the supreme Śakti is not different from the supreme Self.

19.   The burning power of fire is not separate from fire. It is only described as if separate when first explaining it to someone like a child, who does not fully understand the nature of fire.

20.    When you enter the energetic Śakti state[5] and realize the undivided unity of Śiva and Śakti you are truly one with Śiva. So, in this practical context alone Śakti is the doorway or face of Śiva.

21.    Just as the light of a candle or the rays of the sun illuminate the way, in just the same manner Śiva can be discovered through his Śakti, my dearest.

22.    Śri Devi said: Oh Lord of Gods, the god who is symbolically ornamented with trident and skull,[6] please tell me how to reach your true state that is beyond the limitations of time, space and direction. How can one reach this state of fullness that defies description?

23.    How does the supreme Goddess become the face of Bhairava? Oh Bhairava, please tell me all of this in plain language so that I may know it completely.

(The 112 Dharanas begin)

24.    Śri Bhairava said: Prana moves upward and Apana (jiva) moves downward. The supreme Goddess manifests in the two points.[7] Fixing the mind at the two places of origin for the inbreath and the outbreath you will experience this state of fullness.

---

[5] Kundalini.

[6] The trident represents the characteristic expressions of Śiva: will, knowledge, and activity. These are his Śakti. The skull represents his freedom from and mastery of the universe of objects and concepts.

[7] Of the visarga ( : ) This mark in Sanskrit represents an aspirated breathy sound and there is a kind of literary and metaphysical pun being engaged here.

25.    There is a void place between the inbreath and
       the outbreath, between the outbreath and the
       inbreath. In these moments of stillness, in these
       two empty places you will discover Bhairavi and
       the essence of Bhairava.

26.    When the air does not move swiftly in any
       direction, the dichotomizing thought patterns
       disappear, and in the center the form of Bhairava
       manifests.

27.    When the breath has been stopped completely,
       retained inside or outside the body, in this
       tranquil moment the peace of Śakti is revealed.

28.    Moving from the root like scintillating rays of the
       sun, Śakti becomes a more and more subtle light,
       until she dissolves completely at the crown. As
       she dissolves Bhairava manifests.

29.    Rising up in a form like lightning, moving
       through all the chakras one by one to the crown
       until the dawn comes at last.

30.    Pierce the twelve[8] successively with a correct
       understanding of their twelve associated letters,[9]
       from gross sound to subtle sound and the being-

---

[8] These are tantric energy centers somewhat different from the popular
seven chakras. They are: 1. janmagra – the head of the generative organ; 2.
Mula – the root center; 3. Kanda – "cauda equina" the bundle of spinal
nerves near the "tan tien"; 4. Nabhi – the navel; 5. Hrd – the heart; 6.
Kantha – the cavity at throat; 7. Talu – the palate; 8. Bhrumadhya – the
space between eyebrows; 9. Lalata – Forehead; 10. Brahmarandhra – the
apex of skull; 11. Śakti – the pure energy beyond body; 12. Vyapini –
energy beyond which appears when the Kundalini completes its path.
[9] 1. a; 2. ā; 3. i; 4. ī; 5. u; 6. ū; 7. e; 8. ai: 9. o; 10. au; 11. am; 12. ah.

ness beyond sound, liberating yourself one by one until finally you reach the subtlety of Śiva.

31.    Fill your body with breath energy all the way up to the top of your head, free your mind of all thoughts and cross the bridge at the eyebrows to experience the rise of omnipresence.

32.    As if picturing the five colored circles of a peacock's tail, meditate on the voids of your five senses spreading through the universe, becoming immersed in the heart of absolute void.

33.    Gradually, in this way, wherever there is mindful awareness, whether on an empty space, a wall, or a worthy person, you will receive the reward of absorption.

34.    Fixing the attention of your mind upon the interior space of the skull, sitting in a stable position with eyes closed, discover what is eminently discernible.

35.    Focus your meditation on the empty space within the middle channel in the spine, slender as a lotus stem, and the goddess will reveal the divine.

36.    Close the seven openings of your head with your hands, piercing the eyebrow center to merge into the bindu (point of light) that appears in the blocked entrance. Within the bindu the supreme state is discovered.

37.    By agitating your eyes with your fingers a subtle
       flame appears. Hold this bindu at the top of your
       head or in your heart to melt into the infinite.

38.    Master listening with total unbroken concentra-
       tion to the unstruck sounds[10] ever flowing like a
       rushing river within your inner consciousness
       and you will attain to the supreme consciousness.

39.    Perfectly recite the AUM mantra slowly and with
       deep concentration. As the sound fades into
       silence slip into void in the silence of Śakti, Oh
       Bhairavi.

40.    Whoever contemplates the void at the beginning
       or end of any letter or sound will become the void
       by meditating on the void.

41.    By gradually establishing one-pointed attention
       on the sound of stringed, wind or percussive
       instruments over a prolonged period, as this
       finally dies off you will become absorbed in
       omnipresent consciousness.

42.    Also reciting one-lettered mantras moving from
       the gross sound of the letter into more and more
       subtle sounds, as you discover the void within the
       sound through repetition you will become Śiva.

43.    Meditate on your body as a void that extends
       infinitely in all directions at once. When the mind
       is free from thoughts all is dissolved into the
       infinite.

---

[10] Try sticking your fingers in your ears.

44.    When you meditate simultaneously on the void at the crown and the void at the root, by the bodiless Śakti you become the mind of the void.

45.    By steadily concentrating on the void at the crown, the void at the root and the void at the heart simultaneously all thoughts will cease, and the thought-free state of Śiva will arise.

46.    If you concentrate on some part of your body as a void for even a moment, without any thought-constructs, you will be liberated into the thought free state.

47.    Oh gazelle-eyed one, concentrate on the fact that all parts of your body are pervaded by void and your perception will become steady.

48.    Meditate on your body as a wall of skin with nothing inside it. By meditating like this you will find that which cannot be meditated upon.[11]

49.    Close your eyes and center your one-pointed concentration in the middle of the heart lotus. Blessed one, the highest spiritual realization will be achieved.

50.    Dissolve consciousness of the body everywhere into the crown with firm one-pointed practice and the essence of the goal will be revealed.

51.    If you fix the mind on the crown every moment of the day, wherever you are and whatever you are

---

[11] This practice forms a part of the "Completion Stage" in much of Tibetan Tantra.

doing, your mental fluctuations will diminish day by day and an extraordinary state will develop.

52. Concentrate on a fire rising from your toes (or penis) burning up your whole body. When you are utterly destroyed a peaceful state will appear.[12]

53. In the same way meditate on the whole universe consumed by fire. Meditating without wavering or distraction in this way results in the highest human condition.[13]

54. Meditate that the subtle elements all the way to the subtlest elements of your body or the whole universe are being absorbed into their sources. At the end the supreme will be revealed.[14]

55. Having meditated on the breath becoming more and more subtle as you concentrate on the crown, then move your consciousness into the heart to attain freedom and liberation.

56. Meditate on the entire universe gradually dissolving from gross to subtle to that which is beyond subtle until you experience complete dissolution of the mind into pure consciousness.

---

[12] The mantra AUM RA-KSA-RA-YA-UM TANUM DAHAYAMI NAMAH is also associated with this practice.

[13] Advanced adepts may recognize these last two as quite similar to "Advanced Consecration."

[14] It occurs to me that this is somewhat similar to my "Advanced Communion."

57.    Expansively meditate on Śiva consciousness pervading the whole universe in all directions and you will experience the great awakening.

58.    O great Goddess, concentrate on the entire universe as a great void, your mind will dissolve, and you will experience complete dissolution.

59.    Fix your gaze inside an empty jar or vessel, ignoring the containing walls. As the jar disappears your mind will dissolve and you will become completely absorbed.

60.    Fix your gaze upon a barren stretch of land without trees, mountains, or walls. Your mind will dissolve and the fluctuations of thought will end.

61.    Meditate on the space in the center between the knowledge of two thoughts or objects. Abandon both simultaneously and in that middle space reality will arise.

62.    Stop in the midst of any awareness or feeling. Restrain your mind from going on to another. In that moment realization blossoms.

63.    Concentrate on your body and the whole world as one pure consciousness with a one-pointed mind and experience the supreme awakening.

64.    By fusing the inbreath and the outbreath into unity either inside or outside the body you will be able to experience the consciousness of equanimity.

65.   Contemplate that the whole universe and your own body are filled with the Bliss of Self. Through your own nectar of bliss you will become the Supreme Bliss.

66.   O gazelle-eyed one, when something truly surprises you (such as being tickled, seeing a magic or juggling trick, or being caressed by a lover) there arises a moment of the Supreme Bliss that illuminates the essence of things.

67.   Closing all your sensory channels, experience the slow rise of Pranaśakti (breath energy) upwards, feeling a sensation like the crawling of ants. In that moment know supreme joy.

68.   Keep the mind in the middle between the hot joy of sexual contact and the cool joy of sexual release, breathing in deeply, joining your consciousness with the pure bliss of sexual union.

69.   When in sexual union with your lover the excited energy of absorption at the climax is the bliss of Highest Consciousness, the bliss of the Self.[15]

70.   Oh Goddess! Even in the absence of your lover, just fully remembering the joy of kissing, embracing or closeness will cause divine bliss to swell.

---

[15] Numerous prudish translators have commented that these sexual suggestions are meant to be merely illustrative and that they should not be practiced. There is no support for this view in the text itself, which seems to consider all experience as being equally useful for realization. Also see śloka 123.

71.    During any occasion of great joy, such as seeing a friend or relative after a long absence, meditate on the bliss that arises, merging the mind with this bliss completely.

72.    When eating or drinking concentrate on the joy of the taste. Fully immerse yourself in this joy and it will become the Supreme Bliss.

73.    While enjoying song and other sense pleasures immerse yourself totally in the experiences, becoming one with them, and you will ascend beyond the mind.

74.    Wherever your mind finds satisfaction, you need only hold on to that without wavering, because right there is where Supreme Bliss naturally manifests.

75.    In those moments before sleep has arrived, but when you are no longer connected with the outer world of sense objects, when the mind enters this state the Supreme Goddess shines forth.[16]

76.    Gazing on a space dappled with rays from the sun or a lamp, in this place discover the light of your own essential nature.

77.    Practicing Karankini, Krodhana, Bhairavi, Lelihana and Khechari,[17] you will see the supreme attainment dawn.

---

[16] In Tibetan Yoga this is called "The Clear Light of Sleep."

[17] Karankini, Krodhana, Bhairavi, Lelihana and Khechari are tantric mudras. I have seen numerous explanations of these mudras with little agreement. It may actually be that the next five dharanas are intended as explanatory. If so, they are not necessarily in order, though they could be.

78.   Sit on a soft seat, keeping your hands and feet relaxed. In this manner the mind can become full of transcendence.[18]

79.   Sit in a comfortable posture curving your arms in an arch over your head. Fix your mind in the space of the armpits and let your mind become absorbed in peaceful dissolution.

80.   Gaze unblinkingly at any object, transfixing your attention inward. This makes the mind vacuous, and you will rapidly attain the state of Śiva.

81.   Center your consciousness in your tongue, your mouth open and your tongue touching the center of your palate. Mentally pronounce "hah," and dissolve into peace.

---

But the next passages may also just be intended as variations, as so many of these dharanas tend to be. Śloka 81 describes one version of the Khechari mudra that I have seen suggested in other yogic treatises. Elsewhere I have seen it described as a spacious consciousness more akin to ślokas 82 or 57. As for their meanings: A. Karankini – skeleton, B. Krodhana – anger, C. Bhairavi – the goddess Bhairavi, D. Lelihana – flame, E. Khechari – roaming in empty space. These are most consistently represented as: A. a state of repose like death B. tense, wrathful posture while forcefully gathering all the tattvas into the power of mantra. (?) C. Keeping eyes fixed externally while turning attention inwards. D. Considering your own consciousness to be one of "one taste" with the cosmos. B. Dwelling in Śiva consciousness continuously. They are represented as associated with five different classes of yogis: A. jñāna-siddhas, B. mantra-siddhas, C. melapa-siddhas D. śakta-siddhas, E. śambhava-siddhas. Other translators have tried to handle these terms more literally, "Lie down as dead. Enraged in wrath, stay so. Or stare without moving an eyelash. Or suck something and become the sucking." (This last may be because flames "lick" things, or else a dim recollection of the tongue-rolling khechari mudra)

[18] This seems rather similar to the fundamental practice of Zazen.

82.    Sitting on a seat or lying down, contemplate that your body is floating unsupported. Your mind is reduced at once to emptiness and you are freed.

83.    Experience a slow swaying of your body, either in a moving vehicle or while sitting tranquilly. Oh Goddess, then you will experience a flood of divine consciousness.

84.    Gaze continuously at the clear sky with steady awareness. Oh Goddess, at once you will achieve the Bhairava nature.

85.    Contemplate that the entire sky, which is Bhairava, is absorbed in your forehead. Experiencing all as Bhairava you will enter the essence of that light.

86.    Fully knowing that Bhairava exists continuously in waking, dreaming, and deep sleep, you will discover infinite splendor.

87.    Like this, in the middle of the darkest, moonless night[19], contemplating the darkness, you will attain the nature of Bhairava.

88.    Similarly, closing your eyes and seeing that extreme darkness, then even with eyes open in front of you, contemplating the nature of Bhairava you will become one with it.

89.    If you obstruct any sense organ you become introverted. Seizing this moment, the Self becomes illumined in that void.

---

[19] In the dark fortnight of the moon.

90.    Reciting the letter "A" without bindu or visarga,[20]
       then, Oh Goddess, a great flow of wisdom from
       the Supreme Lord arises.

91.    Allow your mind to become vacuous as you
       pronounce a letter ending with "...H."[21] You will
       touch the eternal Divine Self.

92.    Meditate on your own self in the form of a vast
       unlimited expanse in all directions and your
       unsupported consciousness will reveal its true
       nature.

93.    When one of the limbs of your body is pierced
       with something sharp like a needle, there,
       projecting your consciousness right there, you
       move into the pure state of Bhairava.

94.    When you contemplate that there is no real mind
       or ego, this absence of thoughts will free you into
       the non-dual state.

95.    Maya is delusive, and her sheaths cause limited,
       fragmented perception. Understanding this fully
       will end your sense of separateness.

96.    Observe a flash of desire as it springs up and put
       an end to it. Truly ending it, consciousness will be
       absorbed in the source.

97.    Ask yourself, "Before I experience knowledge or
       desire, what am I? I am being in essence!" Become

---

[20] Silently, without any physical or eventually even mental sound.
[21] Visarga, an aspirated "h" such as AH, EH, UH, KH LH, etc.

absorbed until fully identified with being in essence.

98.   In the midst of knowledge or desire, fix your mind there, considering this the Supreme Self. Make the mind one-pointed here, and realize the essence of reality.

99.   Knowledge is causeless, baseless, and deceptive. It does not belong to anybody. Oh dear one, contemplating this way you become Śiva.

100.  The same essential consciousness exists in all bodies, it is not different anywhere. Everything is pervaded by this. With this realization you will transcend relative existence.

101.  Whether in lust, anger, greed, confusion, pride or jealousy, if you still your mind in the midst of any of these the essence of reality will be all that remains.

102.  If you see the whole universe as a magic show, a magical jugglery, or as a mere picture, you will experience bliss.

103.  Dwell neither on suffering nor on pleasure, Oh Bhairavi! Instead know the middle place and only the essence of reality will remain.

104.  Stop your attachment to your own body and contemplate, "I am everywhere," with a firm mind and complete unwavering awareness. In this way you will gain joy.

105. "Knowledge and desire are not just in me. They are in everything, even jars and other objects." Considering this, you are omnipresent.

106. Everybody is aware of objects and subjects, but the yogi is ever mindful of this relationship.

107. Contemplate the consciousness of every being's body as your consciousness. Dropping concern for your own body, in a short time you will be all-pervasive.

108. Let your mind become vacuous, free your self of all thoughts and associations. This is the state of the Supreme Self, the state of Bhairava, Oh gazelle-eyed one.[22]

109. "The Supreme Lord is omniscient, omnipotent, and omnipresent. I am he, I have this Śiva-nature." Firmly asserting this you will become Śiva.

110. As waves rise from water, flames from fire, rays from the sun, so the various differentiated emanations of the universe rise from Bhairava. They are all mine.

111. Whirl your body round and round, then suddenly drop to the ground. As the agitated energy ceases the Supreme State arises.

112. Let your mind become powerless to distinguish objects, through confusion, dissolution, or agitat-

---

[22] Advanced adepts may recognize this as quite similar to "Shedding the Masks."

ed mental energy,[23] and when this disturbance subsides Bhairava will manifest.

113.   Oh goddess, hear the whole of this mystic tradition as I reveal it completely. Simply by fixing the eyes steadily without blinking the highest liberation occurs immediately.

114.   Plugging your ears and sealing the lower opening,[24] meditate on the endless sound within and enter the eternal Self.

115.   At the top of a well, or a deep hole, gaze steadily into the depths. As your mind becomes silent complete dissolution swiftly manifests.

116.   Wherever the mind moves, whether inward or outward, the all-pervasive state of Śiva is there. Where else could it go?

117.   Whatever you experience through your sensory organs, contemplate the experience as the supreme that exists everywhere. Being absorbed, you will attain fullness.

118.   At the beginning and end of a sneeze, when you are frightened, sorrowful, confused, fleeing from a fight, curious, or at the beginning and end of hunger, such states are the external experience of the Supreme Self.

---

[23] What's being described here is a mental dizziness, as opposed to the physical dizziness of the previous śloka.
[24] The anus.

119. At the sight of someplace that stirs up your memories, leave all thoughts and memories aside. Your body will then lose all reference points and the mighty Lord will pervade.

120. Gaze for a moment at any object, then withdraw your gaze from the object. Withdraw your thought and knowledge of the object. Then, Oh Goddess, you become the abode of the void.

121. Through intense devotion when you are detached you will develop intuition. Constantly contemplating this beneficent power[25] you will become Śiva.

122. When you perceive one object all other objects eventually become void. Contemplating this, even though the first object is still known, the mind rests in tranquility.

123. The purity prescribed by those who know very little, who have not experienced Śiva, is not purity at all. There is no purity or impurity for one who is freed from thought constructs and attains real happiness.

124. The reality of Bhairava is everywhere, even in the most ordinary person. When you realize that nothing exists apart from this you will attain non-duality.

125. When you have the same feeling toward friends and foes, toward honor and dishonor, when you

---

[25] sā śaktih śānkari

realize that the Supreme Self is always full, then you will be forever happy.

126.    Do not feel hatred or attachment toward anyone or anything. Freed from attachment and aversion, in the center the Supreme Self unfurls.

127.    Unknowable, ungraspable, void, unimaginable, all this is Bhairava. When this contemplation ends, illumination takes place.

128.    Placing your mind in the eternal, unstructured, omnipresent void beyond all distinctions you will enter the formlessness of non-space.

129.    On whatever your mind dwells, whatever it really is, leave it aside this very moment. Losing all structure your mind will become free.

130.    "Bha" is terror, "Ra" is howling, "Va" is all-pervading. Thus I give my all to the entire universe. By constantly pronouncing "Bhairava" you will become Śiva.[26]

131.    When you realize that you are making statements such as "I am," or "this is mine," and so on, immediately meditate upon that structureless place beyond them.

132.    "Eternal, omnipresent, indescribable, all-pervasive, master of everything," meditating on these

---

[26] Here is a bit of the darker side of Bhairava. But underlying this is an important metaphysical truth. The basis of all differentiated awareness is fear.

words every moment you will attain to the fulfillment of their meaning.[27]

133. The whole universe lacks any essential reality, like a magical show. What essence is there in the magician's trick? When you finally determine that this is so you will achieve peace.

134. How can knowledge and action exist in the changeless and eternal Self? All external objects and experiences are based upon your knowledge of them, therefore this universe is void.

135. Neither bondage nor liberation truly exists to me at all. These are just for the fearful, frightened reflections in the mind, like sunlight reflecting in water.

136. Pain and pleasure exist only to the senses. Detaching yourself from the senses you will withdraw into the reality of the Self.

137. Everything is revealed through your knowledge of it and the Self is the revealer. Since they have the same nature, contemplate that knowledge and the knower are one and the same.[28]

138. Dear one, when the mind, awareness, energy and individuality dissolve, when these four are gone, the Bhairava state arrives.

---

[27] Quite similar in principle to the second part of the "Conscious Communion with Cosmic Consciousness" tool.

[28] Perceiver and perception are identical.

139.   O Goddess, I have just briefly taught you one hundred and twelve ways in which the mind can be stilled, knowing which anyone can become wise.

140.   Anyone who achieves accomplishment in even one of these practices will become the self of Bhairava, whose very words can bless or curse.

141.   Freed from old age, immortal, endowed with siddhis, this master will be loved by all the yoginis and be master among masters.

142.   Liberated while alive, this master is unaffected in worldly activity. Śri Devi said: If this is the true nature of the Supreme Lord...

143.   In establishing a religion, who is to be invoked and what will the invocation or recitation be? Who will be meditated upon? Who should be worshipped? Who will be gratified by that worship?

144.   To whom do we offer homage and sacrifice? How should this sacrifice be accomplished? Śri Bhairava said: Such practices are exterior and pertain only to gross forms of religion.

145.   Constant awareness of the Supreme Consciousness, bringing one's attention to it again and again, this is the resonant essence of recitation, invocation and mantra. This is the only proper method.

146.    An unmoving mind, formless and unstructured is true meditation. Imagining the body, eyes, face or hands of some image of god is not meditation.

147.    Offering flowers or other sacrifices is not true worship. A firm mind established in the non-dual state of the Supreme Void, this is real worship. From this kind of reverence real dissolution occurs.

148.    Becoming established in any one of these practices, whatever the results, day by day experience is developing into fullness. This is the gratification and absolute fullness.

149.    Pouring the elements and the sense perceptions along with the mind itself into the fire of the Great Void, this is a real oblation, using consciousness as the ladle.

150.    Oh Supreme Goddess, The true sacrifice is the absolute release into bliss, destroying all errors and saving all, Oh Parvati.

151.    The true pilgrimage is absorption into this destroying power.[29] Otherwise what worship can there be of this essence? Who is to be worshipped?

152.    The true sacred bath is absorption into the essential nature of the Self that is all-pervasive, autonomous bliss.

---

[29] rudrashakti

153.    The offerings of worship, the transcendent and immanent that is worshipped, and the worshipper are all one. So what is this worship?

154.    Breath comes in and out, curving under the force of will. When the great goddess stretches upward she is the supreme place of pilgrimage, both manifest and unmanifest.

155.    Abide in this sacrifice of supreme bliss, and by the absorption of this goddess you will attain to the supreme Bhairava. When you exhale you make the sound "sa." When you inhale you make the sound "ha." So you are always reciting the mantra "HAMSA."[30]

156.    This mantra of the great goddess is repeated 21,600 times a day, with every breath. It is easily available, except to the ignorant.

157.    Oh Goddess, I have taught you all this that leads to the supreme nectar. It should never be revealed to anyone.

158.    Particularly do not reveal it to a false disciple, one who is negative, cruel, or lacks devotion. It can only be revealed to advanced, heroic souls ready to be free from all thought constructs.

159.    This teaching can be given to devoted students willing to renounce home, country, children, wife and family.

---

[30] Sometimes also referred to as "So'Ham"

160. Initiation should only be offered, Oh Goddess, to those who recognize that these all are fleeting, but that this supreme wealth is everlasting.

161. You may give up even the last of your life energy, but do not give up the supreme nectar of this teaching. Śri Devi said: Oh Great Lord, I am satisfied. I am at peace.

162. Today I have understood the essence of this teaching, and now I know the heart of all the different powers.

163. With that the delighted goddess embraced Śiva.

# Candle Magick Applications for the New Hermetics
## Part One
By Frater Sabriam

## Introduction

Lighting candles is something that many of us do everyday without really thinking about it, with the intention perhaps setting a mood, or making a room smell nice. But the lighting of a candle is one of the most primal magical acts one can perform, stemming from a connection to an age when humankind was awestruck by fire.

Fire was unexplainable, dangerous, and yes, magical. Harnessing that energy was a pivotal moment; learning to create it and use it towards positive ends, rather than being slave or victim to the destructive aspects of fire. However, as fire came more to mean warmth and sustenance, it has never lost its mystical value.

There is a rich history of various forms of magick involving fire. From Shamans and Native Americans dancing and chanting around fires to invoke ecstatic trance, to modern drum circles held around bonfires to achieve much the same thing, and Wiccans lighting candles at Candlemas to call forth spring, fire has held religious and spiritual significance in the way diverse cultures have worshipped. In fact, one of my favorite childhood memories involves a sea of devotional candles in a Catholic church. It was not explained to me the purpose of those candles, but I was instinctually filled with a sense of reverence.

I am compressing history here, but the idea of fire evolved from an essential for survival to the experience of transporting ones prayers, petitions and intentions up to the gods. This is not an inaccurate metaphor, for that is exactly what you are trying to accomplish in performing a ritual using a candle as the focal point. Really, that is all the candle is; a physical representation of your will and intention, announcing those to the Universe.

Introducing candle magick into ones repertoire will be a natural transition for most of you, as most magicians already use altar candles of special import for their working. There are many applications for the NH tools that will make your candle magick much more efficacious and potent than traditional methods. I will outline a few of these below, and explore more applications in part II of this article in the next journal.

## Choosing the Right Candle

The primary consideration when selecting candles is color; the size and type of candle is of secondary importance. The only real determining factor regarding size is the length of the ritual. Will it be 45 minutes or several days? You will also want to use untreated, unscented candles, for as you can imagine, a pungent cinnamon apple aroma could distract from the mood of the ritual, or create dissonance with any incense you have chosen. The color of the candle should be appropriate to the intention of the ritual. The following are correspondences that were a part of a little candle magick 'kit' that I bought years ago, along with some additions of my own.

Red:        Love, passion, energy, enthusiasm, cour-
            age, element of fire, Geburah
Orange:     Strength, authority, attraction, job, success,
            Hod
Yellow:     Clairvoyance, learning, mind, communi-
            cation, the element of air, Tiphareth
Green:      Healing, money, prosperity, luck, fertility,
            Netzach
Blue:       Healing, meditation, tranquility, forgive-
            ness, element of water, Chesed
Lavender:   Intuition, dignity, spiritual shield
White:      Protection, peace, purity, truth, cosmic
            consciousness, Kether
Pink:       Emotional love, friendships, affection, har-
            mony
Turquoise:  Awareness, meditation, moon, creativity
Sea Green:  Emotional healing and protection, calming
Rose:       Self love, enhancing relationships
Black:      Absorption and destruction of negative
            energy, the element of earth, Binah
Peach:      Quiet strength, joy
Purple:     Spirituality, wisdom, psychic awareness,
            Yesod
Navy Blue:  Harmony, understanding, truth
Silver Blue: Deep wisdom, intuition, the moon

You can add to this list any correspondences that seem appropriate to you. These ultimately are suggestions; your inner genius should be your guide.

Once you have chosen your candles, they will need to be dressed with an anointing oil. It doesn't matter if it is an oil that you made yourself, an anointing oil that is purchased, or olive oil. The important thing to remember is that, if the oil has a tint to it, make sure that it is the same color as the candle. Ultimately, whatever is used, it doesn't matter, for when we move on to charge the candle, you will charge the oil as well. My personal preference is olive oil, for two reasons. It's readily available, and it's neutral. Ultimately, whatever is used, it doesn't matter, for when we move on to charge the candle, you will charge the oil as well.

You will also need candleholders, of course, sturdy enough so that they will not topple over, but with a base that is fairly narrow, as there are some rituals that will require two or more candles to practically touch. There are various sizes of narrow based ceramic holders that meet this criterion.

## Safety

When deciding on a space for the altar, safety is of primary importance. Make certain that there are no curtains close by that could catch fire, and again, I cannot overemphasize enough the importance of sturdy candle holders. Also, make sure that your altar is set up where the candles will not be disturbed if you are planning a ritual that takes place over several days. The size of the altar will depend on the number of candles used in the ritual. However, if limited by space, there are still options for using a small altar regardless of the number, which I will discuss in part II.

## Preparation

For the first part of this article, I will provide a very simple ritual that is designed to aid in invoking Communion with Cosmic Consciousness, the Bornless One, the Knowledge and Conversation of the Holy Guardian Angel, or whatever you may wish to call it.

For this ritual, you should have the follow small grocery list of items:

*1 white candle, plus two altar candles*
*Anointing Oil*
*Ritual space*
*You*

The first step is to consecrate the candle, for it is to become as much of a magical weapon as the dagger, cup, pentacle, and censer. Traditional instruction pretty much amounts to 'while dressing the candle, think real hard about your intention'. The technique I am about to discuss is a amalgam of a few NH techniques: at its base, pore breathing, then Creating Artificial Elementals and Projection of Energy to Charge Spaces.

You will want to have available on the altar a white candle, the holder, and the consecrating oil. The altar can be as austere or ornate as you please, but let's assume for now that the accoutrements are very bare-bones. At the very least, there should be two altar candles and the ritual candle and accompaniments. Incense is optional, but since most magicians work with an incense that either anchors them to ritual consciousness, or who use it in correspondence with the operation in question, I would suggest that this pattern remain unbroken.

If you wish to have a more 'magical' altar, I would suggest that you place your elemental weapons in the appropriate quarters, so as to provide a sort of temple-within-a-temple in which to place and burn the consecrated candle.

One last item: you may also place at the top of your altar the image of the god form with which you are most familiar working or with whom you most empathize. For example, I place a small statue of the Egyptian goddess Ma'at, who represents Truth, Justice, and Balance as a subtle reminder of my core principles and of that to which I wish to attain. If you do not currently have such an image, that is perfectly fine, but a recommendation nonetheless.

## Now For the Fun

This ritual is designed to consecrate a candle that will be burned during each of the Communion with Cosmic Consciousness and Bornless One sessions of the NH Adept level, so a good sized taper would be recommended. If you have already advanced through the NH course, and have attained such communion, this would still be a worthwhile exercise from a purely devotional rather than invocational point of view.

Set up your temple space. Arrange the altar as you see fit to do so, and begin relaxing. Light the altar candles and incense. Create the atmosphere in your temple space. Once you are ready, get into the asana that you use in your regular work.

1. Enter the altered state using your meditation anchor, or some other method with which you are familiar.

2. Purification

3. Consecration

4. Casting the Circle/Grounding and Centering

5. Take the candle in hand, visualizing the desired energy as filling the entire universe in a diluted, but all encompassing form. In this diluted form, it is mixed with all other energies. However, become aware of this particular energy by imagining the appropriate color, sound and feeling accumulating as you concentrate on it.

6. Begin pore breathing, drawing the energy of Cosmic Consciousness into you body through all of your pores. Fill yourself with this energy until you feel you feel you could nearly burst. Experience this energy palpably and visibly inside your body, both in your inner temple and in your physical body until you are charged up like a battery.

7. With both hands, hold the candle out in front of you, both in your inner temple and physical world.

8. Allow the energy to move from your solar plexus, down your arms, and into the candle. Make sure that this visualization is as vivid as possible in appropriate color and intensity.

9. Dip your fingers in the consecrating oil (the smaller the candle, the less needed.)

10. Begin rubbing the oil into the candle, from the center out to each end, with the intention of imbuing the candle with the energy raised. (It may be helpful to develop a mantra of some sort, something like "It is my Will to attain Communion with Cosmic Consciousness". As you repeat this, keep absorbing the energy and transferring it to the candle.) See the candle becoming imbued with power, until it is completely saturated.

11. Once you have determined that the candle has been consecrated, place it in the holder, and either continue with the ritual, or perform the Grounding and Centering if you will continue at some other time.

Now, choose your flavor of connection, with either the NH tools of Communion with Cosmic Consciousness or Bornless One; whatever method works best for you. If you consecrated the candle in a separate ritual, light the altar candles and put on the incense. Before the Grounding and Centering, light the consecrated candle. If this is a continuation of consecration ritual, you have already performed the Grounding and Centering, so no need to do it again. Gaze at the lit candle. Focus on communion with cosmic consciousness. Think about attaining that connection. Muse over how ecstatic the union will be, and how far beyond your expectations the experience will be. Commence with the ritual, keeping your eye on the candle as much as you can, but in the areas where other visualizations are called for, at least keep in mind the presence of the consecrated candle.

During the final section of either session as you are rising to merge with Cosmic Consciousness, beginning with "I am the Bornless One..." recitation, or the Communion with Cosmic Consciousness expansion of consciousness, open your eyes and again gaze at the candle, and feel the power of your aspiration flow through you. You may close your eyes again after a short time to work through the visualizations.

Once complete, you may snuff the candle. If you have chosen one large enough, you may use the candle for further sessions, or if you wish, you can light it for a few moments daily as signal of devotion to your Holy Guardian Angel.

The above is a pretty simple example of candle magick, and in part 2 of this article, I will explore some more complex forms, using multiple candles and various setups. From my point of view, the use of candles has added a great deal of an almost romantic angle to my personal work, and I hope you find the same to be true. Feel free to experiment and find your own best uses.

Until the Fall…
Fra. Sabriam

# Enochian Memories
## By Frater Pandokeus

In the early 1990's I found myself living in St. Louis, where I met a group of men and women practicing ceremonial magick after responding to their advertisement of a meet-and-greet at a local metaphysical bookstore. They were a fairly active clan, holding meetings a couple of times a month, and I was eager to learn from them, hear their stories and just generally have people to talk to and ask questions of, as I clumsily explored a variety of esoteric subjects on my own.

At one such meeting, the topic of Enochian magick entered into our group's conversation. I had seen the word 'Enochian' in passing, but for the large part, it was an unfamiliar arena to me, both in practice and general knowledge. One of the older members smugly proclaimed to have practiced Enochian magick, in his past. Excitedly, I asked him to tell me something about it. What was it like? What made it different from other kinds of magick? Was there a personal experience he could share with us, to help illustrate the genre? Sadly, the answer to all of these questions was 'no'. He flat out refused to discuss the subject and became angry, insisting that it was all too personal to discuss. Wait a minute! Wasn't one of the reasons we all regularly gathered as a group, to discuss magick? This was the same group of people with whom I had participated in a goetic-styled evocation of Baez, in the basement of the house of the man in question, no less. I couldn't begin to imagine why he adamantly refused to talk about it. Had he been sexually molested by these Enochian entities? Or, was there something more sinister at work here?

For the next several years I was met with similar refusals of discussion as I traveled, moved around, met new people and continued posing the same kinds of queries. In most instances, the individuals in question seemed slightly hostile when I pushed the issue or quizzed them on the subject matter. Eventually, I came to assume that all of this had nothing to do with their experiences and everything to do with their lack of experience. Luckily, it seemed like no time at all before I would find myself living in the beautiful Pacific Northwest and meeting up with several individuals who could answer all of those questions and more.

One of my first chances at Enochian magick presented itself shortly after I arrived, as I was asked to act as the scribe during an attempt to obtain a talisman in order to secure a temple or some such plan. I was new to both the group and the area, consequently, acting as the scribe in a group setting seemed like the perfect way for me to get my feet wet. I recall not knowing what to expect. I also recall that the experience as a whole was a bit of a let down. I wouldn't call the entire ritual a failure, but our acting scryer spent a fair amount of time unable to navigate his visions, due to the feeling of being trapped and blocked by walls.

Six months would pass before Frater Ixion and I would begin exploring the Enochian realm on our own. We would proceed to spend the next couple of years making regular visits to their etheric land in order to study, document and experiment with these visions.

Admittedly, we didn't start off with much of a plan. Our idea was simply to explore this arcane system of angelic conversation which we both found fascinating. Over time, reoccurring themes and ideas would surface and even if it all never did smooth itself out into a perfectly organized and working universe, no one could say that it wasn't self-contained and brilliantly intricate.

For our first encounter, we drew straws as to who would act as the scryer and who would perform the ceremonials. The prospect of either seemed equally nerve-racking, so at the time it didn't make much of a difference to me that I ended up as the scryer. In retrospect, I'm glad that I was able to go into the entire experience blind, uninfluenced by what would have been my partner's experiences the week before. As it stood, I wasn't sure what to expect. I had nothing to draw on, other than looking on as a voyeur, half-a-year earlier while taking notes of a botched attempt by a member of our group, a memory which had largely faded, if it was even anything substantial to begin with.

Frater Ixion worked laboriously, running about the altar, drawing sigils in the air and sounding out long strings of words in this strange, foreign tongue. All the while I sat with my eyes closed, worried to no end that nothing would happen or even worse, that I would get it wrong! And then he stopped speaking, and I realized that all eyes were on me at this point. Amazingly, my visions started immediately. They were full of color and detail and made no sense whatsoever. But, led with the cautious voice of my magical partner-in-crime, I found myself being guided on an impromptu journey through a bizarre world. Frater Ixion furiously scribbled notes, as I described what I was seeing, occasionally giving me a verbal nudge, to keep me focused or asking questions for elaboration.

When the ritual was over we sat in amazement, staring at each other. Did I just make all of that up? Was all that real? How the hell did that just happen? These were the type of questions which would continue to plague our intellectual minds for years to come. Was this the reason that I was refused answers on the matter back in St. Louis? Was it confusion and self-doubt which left that man guarded from discussion? Perhaps.

As time passed, we became more comfortable moving between our daily "real" world and this other, symbolic one. In fact, the unifying factor over the years always seemed to be that the visions felt like a living language of symbols. The images and settings were almost always primal in nature, or perhaps a better description would be elemental. Sometimes those symbols were spot-on, while at other times they only served to confuse us. In those times of confusion, however, it wouldn't be uncommon for one of us to discover after the fact, that we had made some error in our ritual. Curious.

Frequently we would encounter strange entities who greeted us with cryptic wisdom, and in the end, this was always what we were in search of. It was the conversations which fascinated us. Even while looking past the outward appearance of the beings in question, which varied wildly from place to place, vision to vision, in forms beyond anything we could have imagined, there was always a unity in their manner of speech. There were certainly different personalities, of course, different quirks and habits. Sometimes they were pranksters, and sometimes they were academic in nature. Sometimes they were laborers, while sometimes they seemed myth-ic. Some were happy to entertain our questions while others found us irritating or bothersome. However, through all of it, their speech was always curiously mystical and almost soothing at times. It was one of the things that united them, in an otherwise unpredictable and random world.

As time went on, Frater Ixion and I began to shift our focus from purely exploratory to deciding on a mission before each of the sessions. Sometimes our plan was to request a magical talisman or a piece of magical inform-ation, in which instances we'd have to decide before-hand which of these angels would likely be in posses-sion of such a thing, based on their elemental attributes or relationship to each other. Rarely did these types of missions ever succeed for us. That's not to say that the operation was without a vision, but usually we simply ended up with what seemed like nonsense, rather than something cohesive and useful. I only have a single memory of gaining a working talisman, and in almost every instance of seeking magical information, we only ended up more confused then when we started, which usually resulted in said project crumbling away.

And, in the end, it always came back to the con-versations. Rather than us trying to force something unnatural to happen, our most successful and satisfying sessions were fairly freeform and unscripted. It was almost like a type of psychological divination, in which we would obtain a cloudy piece of wisdom or insight, which after some discussion or meditation suddenly seemed a lot more profound than at first glance. In many ways it's an impossible task to truly explain it with clarity.

Eventually, Frater Ixion and I started to work with and incorporate other local magicians who showed interest in what we were doing. We often used those opportunities as secret experiments of our own, hoping to verify or debunk our own work. Occasionally our novice scryer would receive a weak vision, which was to be expected. At the same time, however, there were numerous occasions in which we would allow the newcomer to scry an angel we had already visited, in hopes of hearing a similar vision to the one we had previously recorded. This type of experiment was frequently met with such positive results that it stopped surprising us.

For a brief period we experimented with choosing random angels to visit or keeping as much information from the scryer as possible. Our concern was that we had become too used to experiencing the visions and even by knowing which element the angel resided in, was allowing our subconscious to influence the magical results. Sometimes we would choose an angel at random by drawing a tarot card and then determine which angel would correspond with those attributes. But, even our attempts to randomize the process or trick ourselves or the scryer, usually failed, in that the visions were still a success.

As the years passed, Enochian became less of a priority, taking a backseat to employment, family and other pursuits. And, in the end, we all slowly moved on, relocating and going our separate ways.

One thing that I find curious is that even though over a decade has passed since that first event, I can still recall the vivid colors and landscape of my initial vision. I've had dreams fade away, often immediately, and as I read through my old dream journals, I frequently have no memory or idea of what I was writing about. So, how is it that I can recall with such clarity the tiniest of details of an event many would claim never happened? Sadly, I can't answer that question, other than to say that for me, those experiences exist in my memory as solidly and as real as my day-to-day life. That's not to say that they didn't happen "between the worlds", as it were, but they most certainly happened. Or, if you wish to ask me what it all means, once again I'm afraid that I can't answer that question. And, in the end, I find myself wondering if maybe that guy in St. Louis knew what he was talking about after all.

# "New," "Highly Exotic," "Eastern" Meditation Techniques
## By Jason Augustus Newcomb

New approaches to spiritual practice are quite popular in some modern circles. The "New" Hermetics is certainly one species of this genus. Some people are always looking for the new, even regularly abandoning their current path entirely for the newest fad. In our consumer culture there are quite a few people who are forever hunting down the latest and greatest new spiritual path. We trade in our laptop computers, cars and cell phones regularly, why not trade in our spiritual belief systems too? This, of course, has its dangers, since we are likely to spend all of our time searching, searching, searching, and none of our time finding.

But innovation is not something that is always appreciated at all in spiritual circles. Being traditional is often viewed as the appropriate way of doing things. "Spiritual" people are often not looking for the newest way to do things, instead seeking the most correct, most legitimate, the "true lineage," in other words the most traditional way of approaching practice. In a lot of the world's spiritual traditions things are being done more or less in the same way that they've always been done going back into the murky recesses of history. This traditionalism is viewed as somehow making the spiritual practice more authentic. I've even experienced a good deal of resistance to my own work on that basis alone.

But in fact it is in large part innovation that sustains the transmission of spiritual knowledge from generation to generation. A closed system of spiritual ideas and practices quickly becomes a mere shell of ossified formalism. It is the innovators who breathe new life and spirit into any system. All fields require new methods and understandings to remain relevant in an ever-changing world. By offering fresh and relevant interpretations of the spiritual path we sustain and renew that eternal flame in every era. As long as we recognize that ultimately all roads lead to the same mountaintop (or at least similar mountaintops), looking at the spiritual practice in new ways can keep it fresh and alive. And more importantly, it can help us to understand and deeply connect with what might otherwise just be an irrelevant historical curiosity. So, we must balance novelty with legitimacy, the old with the new, if we are to sustain legitimate practice and understanding of spiritual awakening.

I regularly discover new and innovative spiritual and magical teachers, mostly through my own prodigal students who come to me enthused about and enamored with some other teacher's work. Rather than feeling too heartbroken about being thrown over for some more glamorous guru, I often like to examine what it is that these other teachers have to offer. I always like to learn new things, new ways of looking at things and new methods for teaching and learning. Some of these teachers offer something really rather revolutionary. Others have just found new ways of covering the same old material in shiny new packaging. Both can be useful. In the next few journals I will probably share some more of the best of these, but in this article I will discuss three simple techniques that I have found quite useful in expanding my own awareness, and in seeing how simply quite dramatic changes can occur in consciousness. Two of them are directly from innovative teachers, and the third is my own interpretation of something that I have seen in the work of several other teachers. These techniques all have a somewhat "Eastern" flavor, but none of them require any shift in your basic outlook, neither eastward nor westward. What I appreciate about these three techniques is that they are very simple, do not require any specific metaphysical belief system, and generally yield positive results on the very first try.

Before getting into the nitty gritty of these techniques I'd like to mention that there are generally two basic approaches to spiritual practice, in whatever form you ultimately package it. Either the practice is concerned with simply observing phenomena as they occur, or it is focused on actively creating a novel experience. The former is based clearly seeing things as they are with greater attention and depth, while the latter is based on specific methods for learning to control consciousness or create new experiences.[31] We see the former in Buddhist

---

[31] This becomes more confused in that there are basically two ways in which spiritual movements view the universe. Either they see the universe as somehow fundamentally flawed, or as fundamentally perfect. There are gradations in this, but the Western metaphysical ethos generally tends toward the former. I recently heard an evangelical state, "We live in a fallen universe." This concept pervades much of Western metaphysics, from alchemy to magick. In such a framework, simply perceiving the "present moment" seems insufficient in comparison to work that intends to

insight meditation, Vipassana, Dzogchen, Mahamudra, in Zen, sensory-based breath awareness, really any sensory-based awareness work, as well as in some of the work of modern "non-dual" authors such as Eckhart Tolle. We see the latter in everything from simple "one-pointed" concentration exercises that attempt to produce a novel state called "samadhi," Kundalini awakening work, visualization training, ritual magic, and in general any content-focused contemplation. Both can lead to similar outcomes, though many meditation gurus purport that the former leads to true enlightenment while the latter leads to bliss states that may only be temporary. Others see it differently. Ultimately the two are fused at a certain level of practice anyway, and that is where genuine enlightenment seems to occur.

The standard New Hermetics program, as outlined in my book of the same title, is largely focused on the latter methods. There are a few exceptions, but the agenda of most of the practices is to organize the mind and to develop concentration leading to transformations, highly blissful and empowered states of mind. Magick in general falls under the same banner for the most part. Even my advanced adept seminar is still largely focused on advancements in concentration, though there are a few exercises that focus on specifically developing greater awareness of the present moment, not the least of which is the instruction in supervising students.

I mention this because two of the techniques discussed in this article, "Big Mind" and "Vibratory Meditation," are more closely linked with the former method. Although they take utterly novel approaches, the focus is on what "is there," rather than on creating something superior. This may be a bit unusual for those who are

---

correct or perfect fallen nature. There is of course a middle path through this mire…

more familiar with active content-driven practices. In fact, they may not seem to be much at all at first glance. But they offer a lot to anyone who takes the time to engage them, and they offer fruits much more quickly than most traditional approaches to such ends. That's why I want to discuss them.

The third method, "The Secret Smile," offers a very interesting variation on certain Taoist practices that I think may be quite useful to anyone who has trouble "running energy" or "opening the chakras" with the techniques I've outlined in my other works. This practice approaches energy work from a very pragmatic perspective, from sensory emotional experience, that will hopefully be of assistance to many of you. It also uses the "microcosmic orbit" or "lesser heavenly circuit," as the coduit for energy, which I think has many benefits above either chakra work or the Western "Middle Pillar" exercise.

All of these techniques can be very easily integrated into your esoteric work and each has something fairly beneficial to offer. I recommend giving them all a try and I think you'll find yourself integrating some part of them into your regular work. You can mix and match a bit in here. I'll let you consider how to approach that. So, let's take a look at each in turn.

## The Big Mind Process

I discovered "Big Mind" after several of my students suggested that I look into the work of Ken Wilbur, to see how his integral philosophy could be fit with the various levels and categories of the New Hermetics. I'd heard of Wilbur, but never examined his work at all until then. A long discussion of my humble little thoughts on Wilbur's strengths and weaknesses will have to be saved for another occasion. But as I was poking around on the internet looking into Wilbur's work I discovered that he had become enamored with a practice called "Big Mind." His enthusiasm was so exuberant and palpable that I felt obligated to take a look at this "Big Mind."

"The Big Mind Process" or "The Big Mind Big Heart Process" is a spiritual technique created by a Western Zen master named Dennis Genpo Merzel Roshi. He has written a book, *Big Mind Big Heart,* teaches workshops, has DVDs, and probably other stuff as well. I believe the process has become quite popular. Interestingly, the core of the technique, a dialectic process, actually comes from some of the same root ideas as parts of the early NLP work. "Big Mind" comes directly from the "Voice Dialogue" techniques of Hal and Sidra Stone who were in turn influenced by Gestalt therapy as was NLP co-creator Richard Bandler.

Briefly, "Voice Dialogue" is a dialectic process that attempts to allow disowned sub-personalities within us to have a voice. The intention is a therapeutic one, to allow us to integrate disowned aspects of our conscious-ness. It is a very simple technique that merely involves asking to speak with a novel part of a person's con-sciousness. For instance, if someone is troubled by people who are "cry babies," the therapist might simply ask to speak with the "cry baby" part of the client. The client would then allow his or her own disowned cry baby-ish part to speak freely, and by giving it voice generally allow the client to understand this tendency in themselves and others more clearly. I'm probably garbling and oversimplifying, but as this is tangential I hope I'll be forgiven.

Essentially the "Big Mind Process" is an application of the same basic principles of "Voice Dialogue" to allow us to gain access both to disowned aspects of our personalities as well as (the generally universally disowned) facets of enlightened awareness.

The technique was created by Merzel after having some troubles in his Zen center and working with Hal and Sidra Stone to resolve them. Later he realized that if this "Voice Dialogue" technique could be used to speak to the various parts of our personalities (dualistic minds) it could be equally applied to communicating with the enlightened parts of our consciousness (non-dual mind).

Enlightened awareness is not off somewhere else. It resides within you right now. It is you. It is just there with a lot of other patterns, tendencies and behaviors that are not generally so enlightened. It should be mentioned that all of these labels are fairly worthless. "Big Mind," "Enlightened Mind," "God," etc. These are all just silly phrases that really describe nothing. There is no enlightened mind. It's an oxymoron. But it makes it easier to talk about, especially within the limits of this technique, so I will continue to do so at both our perils.

Basically this technique allows a person, within a very short period of time, really within an hour or less in most cases, to experience an understanding and an identification with this so-called mind of enlightenment. It doesn't instantly deliver enlightenment really, because enlightenment isn't a state.[32] Enlightenment is simply a word. It is used to describe hundreds of different states and stages on the path of self-discovery by different teachers. Life is a constellation of many different circumstances and experiences. As I grow older and more foolish, enlightenment seems to be as much about simply genuinely experiencing the world without playing games as anything else. But this technique gives you a sense of what enlightened awareness is, a taste of the

---

[32] Although out of laziness and sloppiness I do sometimes refer to it that way.

enlightened mind or "Big Mind" as the creator of this technique calls it, as well as a technique for further exploring this "Big Mind."

The technique allows you to move rather simply and fluidly past the constituent parts of your dualistic mind and into the territory of "non-dual voices." This again sounds a bit self-contradictory, as who does a non-dual voice speak to? But that is irrelevant as this technique is experiential rather than philosophical. And through this technique you will reveal aspects of consciousness that are not parts of your usual ego games, universal parts. Basically, you will get the opportunity to sit in the part of yourself that is perpetually enlightened, the part that is outside the games of life.

The process is also interesting because you will discover many and various different voices within your-self through dialogue. In some cases you may be quite surprised to discover the disowned voices within  your dualistic mind, although that is a side issue within this technique.

The "Big Mind Process" is designed to be used as a dialogue method between a facilitator and a student. The facilitator asks a bunch of questions that lead the student to take on different roles in their psyche, to the exclusion of other roles. The process begins with roles that we all have in our dualistic minds eventually leading up to the role of the non-dualistic mind, our mind of enlightenment. The creator actually defines several different roles of the non-dualistic mind which also has a little irony in it, because the non-dual mind seems like it shouldn't contain a lot of dualities. But the technique is very interesting nonetheless, and I think useful in getting a glimpse of the vast scope of our consciousness and the potentialities that are within it.

## Some of the Dualistic Voices:

The Controller
The Protector
The Skeptic
The Damaged Self
The Innocent Child
The Fixer
The Mind Seeking Enlightenment

## Some of the Non-Dual Voices:

Big Mind
Big Heart
Big Mind Big Heart
The Mind of the Tao

Although the technique is designed for use in a dialectic process, in conversation between two people, you could certainly use the technique on your own once you are familiar with it. It seems like it would be most useful to engage it as a dialogue initially, as he designed it, but it can be easily adapted for solo use once you know the basic principles.

I think the easiest way to get a useful experience of this technique is simply to watch and participate in a workshop that is available in its entirety on youtube.

http://www.youtube.com/watch?v=zT9y1YEUjy0

Or you can just do a search for "big mind" at youtube.com and you'll find it. It is in ten or so separate parts, but you can go through them one after the other quite easily. Just play along with your full attention, and you will have a very interesting experience. Beyond that there are books and DVDs and live workshops available if you want something to do with all that extra money that's weighing down your wallet.

The basic strategy is incredibly simple. The facilitator simply asks to speak to one of the above voices. The student makes a physical bodily shift to help loosen up rigid self-concepts and begins to speak as that voice. No effort is required. Effort is an impediment. Instead the student should just shift and begin speaking. It's important that the student really speak from this voice, identifying as the voice, "I am the damaged self," not describing something second hand such as, "My damaged self is afraid of cookies." This identification will allow a fluidic shift outside of the boundaries of the "self," and facilitate moving into the non-dual voices. The student should identify with the specific voice that is called for, not some other idiosyncratic voice. In other words, "I am the damaged self" is appropriate, but "I am the part of Jason that is damaged by too many cookies," is not. The answers that these "parts" or "voices" give should be simple and broad, though they should also be genuine. But getting too caught up in fancy psychological self-inquiry will derail the whole process. Here's a very simple example.

Facilitator: I'd like to speak to the controller.
Student: (shifting posture) Okay.
Facilitator: Who am I speaking with?
Student: I'm the controller.
Facilitator: What is your job in consciousness?
Student: To be in control.
Facilitator: What do you control?
Student: I control what the self says, thinks, remembers, experiences. I control everything that the self does. It is a full time job.

Facilitator: What else would you like to control?
Student: I'd like to control everything. If I could, I'd control it all, I'd control the whole world.
Facilitator: What frightens you?
Student: Lack of control. That's terrible. Sometimes the self loses control, but I am always there to put the pieces back together. I'm always in control.

And so on. This may all seem a bit silly but it is really surprisingly powerful. Several dualistic voices are allowed a time to speak in turn. Once the student has identified with a number of these the facilitator returns to the controller and gets permission from the controller to let the non-dual voices speak without interference from these other voices.

In the workshop on youtube the first of these is the non-seeking mind, the mind that is not seeking anything. This is a very interesting experience to discover so easily that part of your consciousness that is not trying to accomplish anything.

The facilitator then moves the student into the "big mind." This is accomplished quite easily from the non-seeking mind. From there, several other facets can be explored, Big Heart, the Master, etc. The experience happens quite easily, probably easier than you can imagine. As you become aware that you are the "big mind" you become more universal in scope. What is so remarkable is that within the space of an hour you become very intimately aware of the cosmic scope of your consciousness in an extremely simple way.

The reason this happens so easily seems to be because from the beginning you are disengaging from the illusory "ego." You are engaging consciousness as a conglomerate of parts, and this loosens your attachment to your "limited self," allowing it to be dropped quite easily at the appropriate time. The technique has severe limitations. It is more like taking a tour of enlightenment, a vacation at the enlightenment amusement park, rather than a permanent transformation.

But it is a very useful tour, and well worth the effort. Once you have experienced it once, you will be able to get back to these places quite easily, and perhaps one day you might even buy a nearby condo or time share and spend as much time at the amusement park as you like.

This system uses some Eastern terminology, and has a somewhat Eastern flavor, though only mildly so. "Big Mind," although encountered in some Zen writings, is hardly technical jargon. Still, when I first encountered this material, I wondered if it might be possible to adapt this system into a more Western framework. But I think that's probably unnecessary. You could certainly speak as the Holy Guardian Angel or the Master of the Temple but these concepts are less simple and direct than the concept of "Big Mind." Pretty much anyone could understand the term Big Mind, but the western terms have many different meanings for different people. In fact, even more complex eastern terms such as samadhi, dharana, dhyana, nirvikalpi, etc. are a bit esoteric and difficult to comprehend in comparison to "big mind." This a very simple concept for anyone over three to grasp. Simplicity is one of the most beneficial and useful aspects of this technique. Pretty much anyone can have a fairly profound experience easily with this material.

You probably won't really understand how easy and yet quite profound this process is until you do it. Give it a try.

## The Secret Smile

The second technique that I want to discuss is something called the secret smile created by a teacher named Glenn Morris. He was a well-known martial arts practitioner as well as a college professor and business consultant. Morris experienced an unexpected kundalini awakening in his forties and devoted a great deal of time to teaching an integration of martial arts with energy work and meditation for the remainder of his life. He died in 2006, but there are still a f ew people teaching and expanding on some of his ideas.

One of the central elements of his teaching was something he called the "Secret Smile." His Secret Smile technique is based in large part on the Taoist "Lesser Heavenly Circle" or "Microcosmic Orbit," (to which it forms a precursor) and what Mantak Chia calls "The Inner Smile." Morris seems to have been significantly influenced by the work of Mantak Chia, but he adds something unique to his version of that work. The "Secret Smile" is a simplified version of a combined practice of a simplified microcosmic orbit and the inner smile. He also adds some interesting side ideas into it that I think are useful in a meditative practice.

I haven't mentioned the microcosmic orbit much in my own writings, though I do find it a very useful practice in opening the flow and becoming aware of the movement of internal energies. I did provide a version of it in The Book of Magick Power but it is somewhat lost in the midst of other energy techniques there. In much of occult literature there are two basic ways of approaching energy work. One can either approach it in the "Eastern" way, beginning at the base of the spine and raising energy upwards to the crown, or approach it in the "Western" way, drawing down the divine energy from above through the crown and down into the body. These are simplifications of course, but that is the general view. The microcosmic orbit offers you the chance to work with both directions in the same exercise. It also has the advantage of being circular rather than linear, so you are never abandoning or dissipating the energy you've raised. In most types of energy exercises you will ideally not be losing energy, but because your attention is changing directions abruptly as you conduct your work there is a certain amount of loss. The microcosmic orbit solves this problem more or less by keeping your energy moving in a circle. This gives you the opportunity to build up a fairly good "charge" as you keep accumulating "energy" and moving it.

I do think that it's an extremely useful technique that offers some stuff that the more linear raising exercises can't provide. Rather than just shooting energy through the top of your head you are cycling it through your body. This allows you to dramatically grow the energy you are moving through you, making it a more and more powerful experience rather naturally.

The popular western "middle pillar" exercise does in fact contain some "cycling" of "energy" at the end of the practice, but this is most likely an insertion on the part of Israel Regardie, who was himself a student of the Chinese "Secret of the Golden Flower."

The Chinese method also includes a convenient storage method. As you accumulate energy you "bank" a certain amount of it in your "belly cauldron," where you store it for future use. You can also eventually store energy in your "heart cauldron" and your "mind cauldron." There is a complex metaphysics to these exercises in Chinese teachings, involving the transformation of seminal essence (ching or jing) into chi (energy), and then further refining chi into shen (spirit).

Morris' method dispenses with any real metaphysics at all. His technique instead focuses on five feeling states that he identifies as the "natural state" for humanity, the "youthful bliss" that we tend to lose over the course of life. These states are:

Relaxation
Confidence
Laughter
Love
Sexual Bliss

The basic idea is that in Chinese meditation one of the things that you do is to smile into all of the organs of your body, to give them positive energy, to allow them to heal and to become stronger. The basic practice is simply to send the energy of a smile into each of the organs of your body. Glenn Morris instead offers a five-pronged version of this inner smile, involving not just sending the energy of a smile, but these several nuanced energies throughout your body. He also combines this practice directly with a version of the microcosmic orbit itself, so that you are circulating these energies throughout your whole being.

The technique is fairly moving if you put your whole focus into it, and engage each of the states completely. It creates a calm, relaxed, blissful and focused state. The following instructions are my version of this exercise, you can examine Morris's precise directions in his books:

1. Begin by taking up a meditative posture with your spine relatively straight and upright. This can be

done in a chair or on a meditation pillow if that
seems best to you. Morris makes a big point of
stressing the importance of a quiet mind. Try to clear
and focus your mind on the task at hand.

2.  Gently place your tongue on the roof of your mouth.
    (Morris is quite adamant about this)

3.  Breathe deeply and slowly.

4.  Smile. This is important as it sends pleasure impulses
    throughout your being.

5.  Let a current of relaxation move up from your feet,
    through your legs, up your spine to the top of your
    head. Now let that relaxation curl over your head
    and move down the front of your body to your belly.
    Circulate this relaxation energy a few times, letting it
    rest in the belly when you are done. You can link this
    with the breath if you wish, but don't become
    distracted. I like to draw energy up with the
    inbreath, and let it circle downward with the
    outbreath. It may take some experience to get to this
    point. Just move at your own pace. But settle the
    energy in your belly when you're ready to move on
    to the next step.

6.  Now think of a time when you did something very
    well, and others appreciated you for it. Think of a
    time when you felt very capable, effective and
    confident. Then remove the context, just holding on
    to the felt sense. Starting at your feet again, circulate
    this feeling up your spine and then down to your
    belly. (Morris also suggests swallowing your saliva at
    this point, sending the energy down with the spit).

Let it combine there with the relaxation, and circulate both mingled together a few times.

7.  Repeat this same process with a feeling of hilarious laughter, a feeling of deep love (both loving and being loved), and finally the most intense orgasmic feeling you can experience. Circulating all of these mingled energies should feel very good.

8.  Once you've done this, you can solidify these feelings into a small globe of intensely good feeling light, and begin to circulate this around you in the microcosmic orbit. (This is circulating energy around from the groin up through the spine to the head and back down the front of the body).

9.  Draw additional energy into this ball up from your genitals and the earth as it passes your genitals and starts moving up your spine again. Draw more energy in from above as the energy reaches the crown, and starts to go back downward. See how amazing you can make it. You can make it pretty amazing!

10. When you are finished, store this energy in your belly cauldron, the lower tan tien, located a few inches below your navel, and a few inches inside your body. This is the central pivot point of your body. Swirl the energy around in there a few times, spinning it clockwise and counterclockwise to settle it into place.

This exercise will massively increase your overall sense of energy in your body, as well as producing a pleasant, blissful joy for life. In doing this exercise, don't become too concerned about the specific "color" of these emotional feeling states. There may not be that much of a felt difference between laughter and love, relaxation or confidence. As long as it feels good, go with it. Getting all stuck on getting things right is completely counter to the goals of this exercise. Just try it and enjoy.

## Vibrational Meditation

The third technique that I want to discuss isn't really necessarily a "new" innovation. But it is a practical tool that may be quite useful in your work, and a number of the more "innovative" spiritual teachers have mentioned it in their writings and teachings. This technique is often called "shaking" or "vibrational meditation." This kind of practice has a rather long history with many byways and independent developments. Ritual dance, which often takes on a shaking character, has been a part of primitive religious and magical practice for millennia. Many spiritual traditions, from both the East and the West, contain shaking practices, including some within the fairly recent Christian(-ish) movements the Quakers and the Shakers. There are some variations in the techniques, but in principle they are all fairly similar. I'm going to outline both a standing and a seated version of this sort of consciousness altering technique

There are a number of modern authors who have discussed one variation of this technique or another. Probably the most famous of these is (the rather infamous) Bhagwan Shree Rajneesh, (AKA "Osho" and other names) the self-styled guru and ultimately personality cult leader. He was rather well thought of early on in his career, gaining a large following for his teachings, lectures and writings both in India, the United States and around the world. For Rajneesh, a shaking practice formed the initial part of his four part kundalini meditation technique. Each stage was (or is) conducted for fifteen minutes, with musical accompaniment. The first stage of this dynamic method of meditation involved shaking, the second dancing around freely, the third seated or standing in a witnessing state, and the fourth laying down bit. The purpose of the shaking was to free yourself of all the tensions, knots and impediments within your body. That is really one of the most important things that shaking meditation has to offer, freeing you from stresses and tightness, allowing the body to become free.

But it offers much more. A properly conducted shaking session will awaken a profound bodily bliss within you. Apparently it also has a significant effect upon the parasympathetic nervous system that can be extremely healing, resulting in relaxation, release of toxins and a generally buoyant positive sense.

Another author to discuss shaking meditation was Jan Fries who wrote an entire book on shaking practice called Seidways. I think Fries is actually one of the most interesting occult writers of the latter twentieth century, And Seidways is one of the most interesting. Fries proposes that the shaking meditation can be used to enhance any number of magical operations including visionary work and energetic transformation. I will let you examine his book for ideas on these more magical applications. He doesn't get that specific, so prepare yourself to have to get creative.

The specific shaking technique that he gives is fairly identical with that of Rajneesh. There are a few other teachers engaged in shaking meditation practices, including some of the students of Glenn Morris who have continued his work after his death, calling it "skeletal shaking."

The actual instructions are the simplest of these three. I will give two versions, one for a standing shake, and one for a seated one.

## Standing

1. Stand with feet about shoulder width or perhaps a bit wider apart. Allow your knees to bend slightly.

2. Quiet or silence your mind, focusing on the felt sense of your body.

3. Allow your legs to slowly begin shaking. You may have to jump start the process with a small effort, but the shaking should basically continue more or less on its own once you start it. A small bounce of your knees will get things going.

4. Allow the shaking to do what it will, let your body relax into the shaking. It may bob or sway. Your arms may jerk or contort. Just witness it all. Let your body do what it wants to do. Try to just let the shaking continue to do what it needs to do. You may find it becoming more powerful, or settling into a throb. Just do what feels freeing.

5. Continue in this anywhere from ten minutes to a half hour.

6. At the end, sit down and continue silently witnessing for another ten to twenty minutes.

## Seated

1.  Sit on the edge of a chair, legs comfortably splayed outward, your spine straight but relaxed. Rest your hands on knees or in a fun mudra if you have one.

2.  Quiet or silence your mind, focusing on the felt sense of your body.

3.  Lift your heels into the air, keeping the balls of the feet on the ground. Allow your legs to slowly begin shaking. You may have to jump start the process with a small effort, but the shaking should basically continue more or less on its own once you start it.

4.  Allow the shaking to do what it will, let your body relax into the shaking. It may bob or sway. Your arms may jerk or contort. Just witness it all. Let your body do what it wants to do. Try to just let the shaking continue to do what it needs to do. You may find it becoming more powerful, or settling into a throb. Just do what feels freeing.

5.  Continue in this anywhere from ten minutes to a half hour.

6.  At the end, set down your heels and continue silently witnessing for another ten to twenty minutes.


One thing that is highly interesting about this technique is that you may feel quite ecstatic while you are doing it, but when you finish you will definitely feel an incredible blissful flow of energy within you if you sit or lie down, relax, and experience. This will last anywhere from five minutes to another half hour or so.

Does this practice accomplish anything other than this pleasant blissful state? Only continued practice will tell you. The key here is to be in a highly observant but quiet state. There is a transformation in your whole nervous system taking place.

Even if all you ever get out of any of these practices is a sense of bliss and openness the effort was well worth it. All of the above practices can be fairly easily integrated into your New Hermetics work, whether you are just getting started or are working at the adept level. I hope you'll take the time to give them a try!

# Talismans and Pantacles in New Hermetics Practice
By Frater Uraeus en Djehuti

Do what thou wilt shall be the whole of the Law.

Hermetic Magick has a long and venerated history of the use of talismans and pantacles in the performance of its rites. *The Key of Solomon the King, The Magus,* and many other celebrated texts bear witness to this history and give us some documentation of the place this aspect of the Hermetic Science has occupied in the lives of magicians in previous centuries and millennia.

Modern Chaos Magick has also contributed to this occult science and given us the tradition of Sigil Magick which has ancient precedence in such celebrated and well known works as the *Enchiridion* wherein we see sigils of the four elemental archangels derived from the English letters of their names.

The New Hermetics has shown us that it does not take extensive knowledge of foreign languages and ar-cane correspondences to effectively work talismanic magick. The use of any piece of paper inscribed with a properly created Sigil can be effectively charged to work miraculous effects by any magician who has taken the time to learn and practice the process outlined in Jason's revolutionary book *The New Hermetics*. Those who have taken the time and effort to participate in the New Hermetics Supervised Course with its *New Hermetics Training Manual and Workbook* and extremely useful CD Recordings will vouch that this magick works and often works wonders, though sometimes these aren't apparent until time has revealed their miracles.

In the *New Hermetics Training Manual and Workbook* the Student is introduced to a variety of Hebrew words and planetary squares. The allusion is made in the section on talismanic magick that these can be used to construct talismans along more traditional Qabalistic lines although this is not necessary for either effectiveness or utility.

At least one student has explored these possibilities and found that painting them took far too much time and effort. To save time and effort this student rendered the finished designs digitally so that they could be printed out easily and employed in magical purpose. Representations of these talismans accompany this article. These talismans represent various occult forces symbolically and are conveniently blank on the reverse side so that the student can draw the sigil they have created for the purpose the Talisman is to be charged for.

The design of the talismans employs alchemical sigils, appropriate names in Hebrew and Enochian, and in the case of the planetary talismans the planetary square. The traditional colors used in making talismans for Hermetic magick are derived from a diagram known as the Tree of Life represented as the "Minutum Mundum" which uses the colors from Crowley's Queen Scale for the Sephirot and the colors from Crowley's King Scale for the Paths or Netivot and which represents the Tree of

Life in the Human Aura and within the expanse of natures Twenty-One Influences. The Flashing Colors appropriate to the Force represented are used to form the Talismans and are derived from the Paths appropriate to the Force and are as follows...

Planetary.

| | |
|---|---|
| Saturn: | Purple Background with Yellow-Orange Symbols, Letters, and Numbers. |
| Jupiter: | Violet Background with Yellow Symbols, Letters, and Numbers. |
| Mars: | Red Background with Green Symbols, Letters, and Numbers. |
| Sol: | Orange Background with Blue Symbols, Letters, and Numbers. |
| Venus: | Green Background with Red Symbols, Letters, and Numbers. |
| Mercury: | Yellow Background with Violet Symbols, Letters, and Numbers. |
| Luna: | Blue Background with Orange Symbols, Letters, and Numbers. |

Astrological.

| | |
|---|---|
| Aries: | Red Background with Green Symbols, and Letters. |
| Taurus: | Red-Orange Background with Blue-Green Symbols, and Letters. |
| Gemini: | Orange Background with Blue Symbols, and Letters. |
| Cancer: | Yellow-Orange Background with Purple Symbols, and Letters. |
| Leo: | Yellow Background with Violet Symbols, and Letters. |

Virgo:  Yellow-Green Background with Red-Violet Symbols, and Letters.

Libra:  Green Background with Red Symbols, and Letters.

Scorpio:  Blue-Green Background with Red-Orange Symbols, and Letters.

Sagittarius:  Blue Background with Orange Symbols, and Letters.

Capricorn:  Indigo Background with Yellow-Orange Symbols, and Letters.

Aquarius:  Purple Background with Yellow Symbols, and Letters.

Pisces:  Red-Violet Background with Yellow-Green Symbols, and Letters.

Elemental.

Spirit:  White Background with Black Symbols, and Letters.

Fire:  Red Background with Green Symbols, and Letters.

Water:  Blue Background with Orange Symbols, and Letters.

Air:  Yellow Background with Violet Symbols, and Letters.

Earth:  Black Background with White Symbols, and Letters.

The names found on the pantacles are common in Western occultism and most can be found in works like *Godwin's Cabalistic Encyclopedia* and Jason's *Practical Enochian Magick*. As for the names indicated in the Hebrew and Enochian languages they are angelic in nature and are positioned as follows...

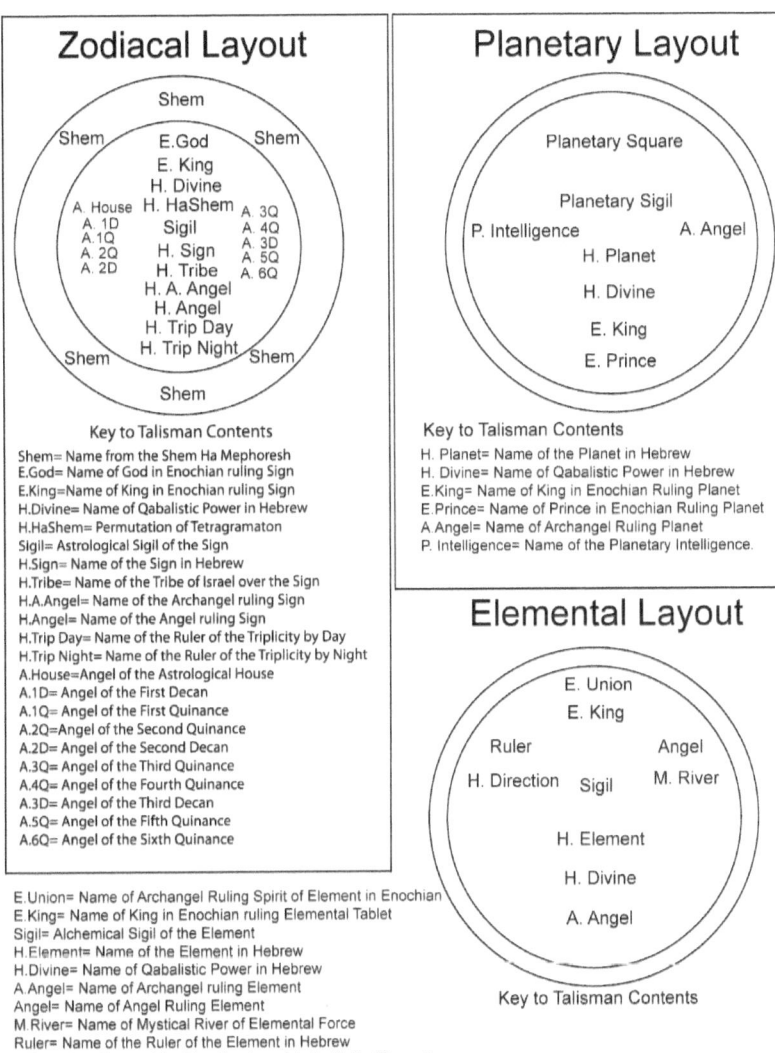

### Zodiacal Layout

Shem
Shem   E.God   Shem
E. King
H. Divine
A. House  H. HaShem  A. 3Q
A. 1D        Sigil       A. 4Q
A.1Q                      A. 3D
A. 2Q      H. Sign    A. 5Q
A. 2D      H. Tribe   A. 6Q
H. A. Angel
H. Angel
H. Trip Day
Shem  H. Trip Night  Shem
Shem

**Key to Talisman Contents**

Shem= Name from the Shem Ha Mephoresh
E.God= Name of God in Enochian ruling Sign
E.King=Name of King in Enochian ruling Sign
H.Divine= Name of Qabalistic Power in Hebrew
H.HaShem= Permutation of Tetragramaton
Sigil= Astrological Sigil of the Sign
H.Sign= Name of the Sign in Hebrew
H.Tribe= Name of the Tribe of Israel over the Sign
H.A.Angel= Name of the Archangel ruling Sign
H.Angel= Name of the Angel ruling Sign
H.Trip Day= Name of the Ruler of the Triplicity by Day
H.Trip Night= Name of the Ruler of the Triplicity by Night
A.House=Angel of the Astrological House
A.1D= Angel of the First Decan
A.1Q= Angel of the First Quinance
A.2Q=Angel of the Second Quinance
A.2D=Angel of the Second Decan
A.3Q= Angel of the Third Quinance
A.4Q= Angel of the Fourth Quinance
A.3D= Angel of the Third Decan
A.5Q= Angel of the Fifth Quinance
A.6Q= Angel of the Sixth Quinance

### Planetary Layout

Planetary Square

Planetary Sigil

P. Intelligence          A. Angel
H. Planet
H. Divine
E. King
E. Prince

**Key to Talisman Contents**

H. Planet= Name of the Planet in Hebrew
H. Divine= Name of Qabalistic Power in Hebrew
E.King= Name of King in Enochian Ruling Planet
E.Prince= Name of Prince in Enochian Ruling Planet
A.Angel= Name of Archangel Ruling Planet
P. Intelligence= Name of the Planetary Intelligence.

### Elemental Layout

E. Union
E. King
Ruler                    Angel
H. Direction   Sigil   M. River
H. Element
H. Divine
A. Angel

E.Union= Name of Archangel Ruling Spirit of Element in Enochian
E.King= Name of King in Enochian ruling Elemental Tablet
Sigil= Alchemical Sigil of the Element
H.Element= Name of the Element in Hebrew
H.Divine= Name of Qabalistic Power in Hebrew
A.Angel= Name of Archangel ruling Element
Angel= Name of Angel Ruling Element
M.River= Name of Mystical River of Elemental Force
Ruler= Name of the Ruler of the Element in Hebrew
H.Direction= Name of the Direction Associated with the Element.

**Key to Talisman Contents**

## Planetary.

The planetary square is topmost on the talisman. Directly beneath the square is the alchemical sigil of the planet. Directly beneath the alchemical sigil is the name of the planet in Hebrew and in Hebrew lettering.

Directly beneath the name of the planet is the Atzilutic
or Qabalistic name of power relating to the planet, also
in Hebrew. Below the Atzilutic name are in order from
top to bottom the names of the Enochian king and Enochian prince who have dominion over the Planetary
Force in the Enochian lettering.

To the right of the alchemical sigil is the Briatic or
archangelic name relating to the planet. To the left of the
alchemical sigil is the Yetziratic or angelic or intelligence
name relating to the planet. The end result is that the
talisman is a fairly complete symbol of the represented
Force from the perspective of Hermetic Qabala.

## Astrological.

The astrological talismans have a series of six names
of three letters arranged in the outer ring of the talisman
according to the shape of a hexagram. These are the
names which relate to the astrological sign of the Shem
HaMiphoresh or seventy-two fold name of Hermetic
Qabalistic renown.

Topmost of the names within the inner circle of the
talisman is the holy name relating to the astrological
sign from the Enochian elemental tablets, this name is in
Enochian lettering. Beneath the Enochian holy name is
the name of the Enochian king presiding over the force
the Sign represents, this name is also in Enochian lettering. Beneath the name of the Enochian king is the
Atzilutic or Qabalistic name of power relating to the
astrological sign, given in Hebrew. Below this Atzilutic
name is a permutation of Tetragrammaton relating to
the sign, Tetragrammaton (HaShem in Hebrew) is of
course the Name which provides the basis of Hermetic
work until the level of adept is reached in Hermetic
Qabala each letter representing one of the four alchem-

ical elements. Beneath the permutation of Tetragrammaton is the alchemical sigil of the astrological sign. Beneath the astrological sigil is the name of the sign in Hebrew and in Hebrew lettering. Beneath the name of the sign is the name of the ancient tribe of Israel associated with it according to the attributions of some of the nineteenth century Freemasons. beneath the tribe is the Briatic or archangelic name relating to the sign. Beneath the archangelic name is the Yetziratic or angelic name governing the sign. beneath the angelic name is the name of the "Lord of the Triplicity by Day". Beneath the previous name is the name of the "Lord of the Triplicity by Night".

To the left of the astrological sigil is a column of five names. The topmost name in the left hand column is the name of the angel governing the house with which the sign has been traditionally associated in the science of astrology. Beneath this name is the name of the angel of the first decanate of the sign. Beneath this name is the name of the angel of the first quinance of the sign. Beneath this name is the name of the angel of the second quinance of the sign. And ending the left hand column is the name of the angel of the second decanate of the sign.

To the right of the astrological sigil is a column of five names. the topmost name in the right hand column is the angel of the third quinance of the sign. Beneath this name is the name of the angel of the fourth quinance of the sign. Beneath this name is the name of the angel of the third decanate of the sign. Beneath this name is the name of the angel of the fifth quinance of the sign. And ending the right hand column is the name of the angel of the sixth quinance of the sign. The end result is that the talisman is a fairly complete symbol of the represented force from the perspective of Hermetic Qabala.

## Elemental.

topmost on the elemental talismans is the name of the Enochian spirit from the tablet of union which governs the spiritual aspect of the elemental force according to tradition; this name is given in Enochian lettering. The name which follows in descending order is the name of the Enochian king ruling the tablet with which the element has been traditionally associated. For example the southern tablet for the element of fire and so on. Beneath these Enochian names is the alchemical sigil of the element. Beneath the sigil is the name of the element in Hebrew and in Hebrew lettering. Beneath the name of the element is the Atzilutic or Qabalistic name of power relating to the element, given in Hebrew. beneath the Atzilutic name is the Briatic or archangelic name relating to the element.

To the left of the sigil is a column of two names. Topmost in the left hand column is the name of the angelic ruler of the element as distinguished from the elemental ruler of the element which is a completely different entity. Beneath this name is the name of the direction with which the element has been traditionally associated in Hermetic Qabala. This name is given in Hebrew and in Hebrew lettering.

To the right of the sigil is a column of two names. Topmost in the right hand column is the name of the angel ruling the element. Beneath this name is the name of the mystical river of force pouring into nature from another dimension. These rivers have been ascribed the names of four rivers listed in the Judeo-Christian Book of Genesis where they are described as flowing out of Pardesh or the Garden of Eden. The name of the mystical river is given in Hebrew lettering.

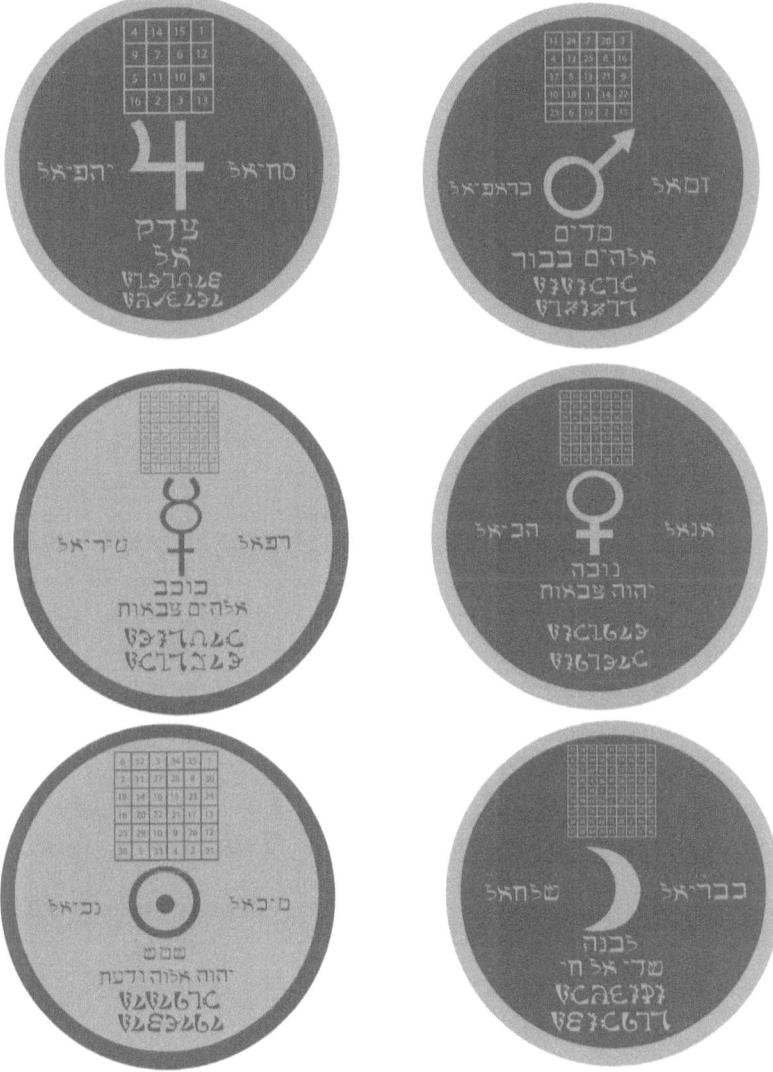

Throughout the span of recorded history magicians have used ritual tools to help them quickly and efficiently wield the occult forces of existence to cause change to occur in conformity with their will. Since at least the advent of what we know as the Ancient Egyptian Civilization these have included a wide assortment of wands constructed in harmony with various symbol structures. The practice of using ritual wands also continued in the era of medieval magicians.

The Freemasons of the nineteenth century and several fringe masonic groups such as the Societas Rosicruciana took the use of ritual wands to heights seldom seen before. Due to the large size of Masonic Halls they were able to construct wands nearly the size of modern baseball bats brightly painted and wielded in elaborate rituals. Many of these wands are beautiful symbols marvelous to behold.

The use of ritual wands is often somewhat inconvenient for modern magicians deprived as they frequently are of the masonic halls or forest glens where their predecessors worked their wonders in days gone by. Some modern magicians have found that the reason some of the wands developed by nineteenth century masons for use in Hermetic Magick approximated the size of a modern baseball bat is because they required such tremendous size to hold according to the symbolic use without crippling hand cramps seriously distracting the Ruach (more or less the Conscious Mind) of the magician from the task at hand.

At least one modern magician has constructed a lotus wand (a wand used to control and direct sephirotic, planetary, elemental, and other occult forces in ritual magick) of the traditional Golden Dawn Variety using a copper pipe the length of the arm, painted appropriately and capped with a lotus cut from aluminum plates. Though this wand was significantly lighter than an identical wand this magician had made from wood it still caused tremendous difficulty in ritual. The previously mentioned hand cramping occurred and additional difficulty removing it from inside the altar and un-wrapping (magical implements are traditionally wrapped in silk to avoid banishing the energies evoked in the charging) the wand while in a magical circle not nearly the size of a masonic hall was noted to some dismay and consternation.

An effective means to circumvent the problems which confront many modern magicians in their attempts to use traditional magical implements is found echoing from the great occultist Eliphas Levi's book *Transcendental Magic* wherein he describes the use of pantacles as a means for efficiently directing the will. In this book Levi describes a pantacle as a complete symbol of the force in question. This definition it is hoped can be said to apply to the talismans outlined in this article.

To use a fire pantacle in place of the well known Golden Dawn fire wand simply construct the talisman and a sigil stating how it will be used according to the methods outlined in Jason's book *The New Hermetics*. Then charge the pantacle with red fiery energy imbued with your purpose. It would not be a bad idea to glue the pantacle to a small coaster or plate to avoid it blowing off the altar during ritual. The pantacle can then be charged exactly as the fire wand would be using a Ritual similar to that outlined in Regardie's book *The Golden Dawn* or one created for that purpose using the information in Jason's *The Book of Magick Power*. This method could be applied to all of the talismans listed here giving a magician a fairly complete set of magical tools.

As an interesting side note, because these pantacles include long lists of angelic names they could possibly be used in one phase of the Abramelin working often overlooked when discussing this procedure. The phase of the operation referred to is of course the convocation of the good and holy spirits. It is not inconceivable that a magician working the program outlined in Jason's book *21st Century Mage* could construct a ritual evocation of the angels on these pantacles using the procedures for evocation to visible appearance given in Jason's *The Book of Magick Power*. This would then add some very interesting experiences to the working and hopefully enrich the life of the magician so inclined.

Another alternative to physical ritual to obtain the convocation of the good and holy Spirits would be to use Jason's CD "Communicating With Angels" available from the Center of Changes. All that would be required to do this would be to have at hand a list of angelic beings to work with (which can be obtained from Jason's *The Book of Magick Power* for example) and to use it on the appropriate days of the traditional Abramelin working.

It is at least interesting to consider the possibility of alternatives to the traditional arsenal of ritual magick using something which is perhaps more convenient to use and store than the objects we are exposed to in such monumental and awe inspiring works as have been given to us by the orders of yesteryear and the ponderous and oft excruciating ordeals some of them would impose on aspirants toward the L.V.X.

Love is the law, love under will.

# The Hero's Journey
# Tarot Spread
by Jason Augustus Newcomb

I am not the first person to stumble across the idea of a "Hero's Journey" Tarot spread. It's too good an idea, too simple, and too perfect. In fact, I just poked around on the internet as I'm writing this and I saw that there are a couple of people who have created similar spreads, and even a woman offering to sell the Hero's Journey to you through the tarot in about ten different ways. I also note that a Llewellyn book called *Tarot for Writers* has just come out, which probably makes reference to some of the things I'm about to talk about. I haven't read the book. I'm just assuming.

At any rate, I've long been a fan of Joseph Campbell, and I recently read Christopher Vogler's wonderful creative writing manual *The Writer's Journey*, which painstakingly analyzes Joseph Campbell's hero myth structure from *The Hero With a Thousand Faces* to help writers (particularly screenwriters) align their creations with this story paradigm. As I read the book it suddenly occurred to me that this structure would make a wonderful tarot spread. The spread actually shares a number of similar card positions with the popular "Celtic Cross" spread, but it organizes them into a more satisfying story line that I feel makes a reading flow more dramatically and interestingly. I've actually been using a spread rather similar to the one I'm about to go over for years, but the "hero's journey" paradigm makes it a bit more precise than what I've been doing.

The New Hermeticist is a goalsetter. Each of these goals is a "hero's quest" set in motion. Using the Hero's Journey Tarot Spread can help you to understand the process you are beginning with each goal, the challenges before you, and some of the steps you need to take to get there. The basic steps in the Hero's Journey pattern as laid out by Vogler are:

1. The Ordinary World
2. The Call to Adventure
3. The Refusal of the Call
4. Meeting with the Mentor (supernatural aid)
5. Crossing the First Threshold
6. Tests, Allies or Enemies (road of trials)
7. The Approach
8. The Ordeal
9. The Reward
10. The Road Back
11. The Resurrection
12. The Return with the Elixir

This spread represents a process from beginning to end, and is well-suited for questions about the big projects and adventures of your life. Let me go over how to use it, and a bit about oracles in general.

There are a few different ways you can lay the cards out for this spread, from a straight line, to a set of rows, to a circle, but I tend to prefer the circle layout as it emphasizes the cyclical pattern of all adventures the best. This layout is based upon a diagram at the beginning of Vogler's book.

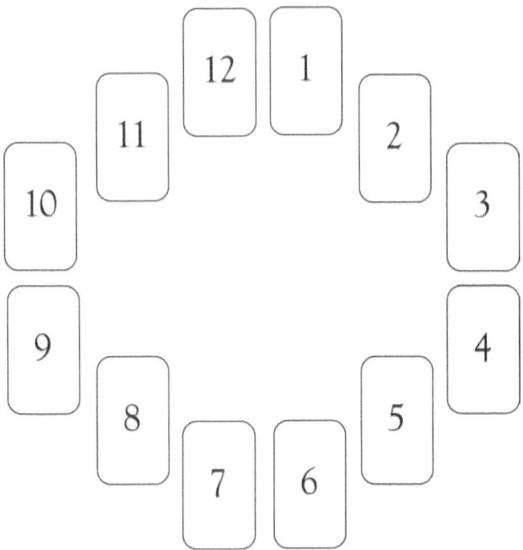

In this lay out the cards travel around and come back to the start again at the end. This fits rather well with the theme of the hero's journey that I'll describe briefly below.

To begin with, you may wish to choose a card to represent you as the "hero." Many people choose one of the court cards based upon physical resemblance or astrological correspondence. But you could also choose one of the major arcana that exemplify the nature of your personal quest. For instance if your question re-gards money you might choose "The Wheel of Fortune." If your question is magical you might choose "The Magician." Your own creativity can provide an infinite number of variations. Some people omit this step entirely. It's up to you.

Once you have chosen a card to represent yourself (if you are doing so) there are two ways of proceeding.

Either you can keep this card out of the deck and begin to shuffle, or you can leave the card in the deck and shuffle. You can cut the deck one or three times or whatever method suits you. At any rate, eventually you will decide you are done and then you will lay the cards out in the above pattern.

If you have left your personal card in the deck you can begin to look for it, and once you have found it lay the next twelve cards in the deck out for your reading. This can be an enjoyable method as it allows your card to "choose" where the journey begins. Of course you don't have to proceed this way.

It should be kept in mind that the specific cards that come up are less important than your reaction to them. The real magick in divination comes from inside you. It is your reaction to the cards that indicates the real circumstances that surround you, and those that are within you.

For instance, if you play around with the Tarot for long enough you will eventually come across the nine and ten of swords, or the tower, etc. These are considered to be pretty much the worst cards in the deck and represent disastrous circumstances. Doom, failure, ruin, and so on. All the nasty stuff. Seeing these cards might make you feel that your efforts are wasted and your hero's journey is destined for failure.

But they are actually a tremendous opportunity to become conscious of circumstances in your life or in your own consciousness that threaten to hurl you over the cliff. What is the "nine of swords" in your life right now? This is the real magick of divination. It gives us the opportunity to use these cards as mirrors into our lives. Which particular ones come up and in what sequence in any reading is really rather secondary. An entirely bad spread does not necessarily indicate failure, it is simply the sequence of cards of cards that came up for you to look at. If you shuffled them up and asked the same question you'd get different cards. Both would be equally valid for interpreting your situation because they are all mirrors that resonate with something in your life. The same is equally true of an entirely positive reading. It doesn't necessarily mean "guaranteed success," it merely means that there are a lot of great energies for you to look at in your consciousness as well.

But from the perspective of a universe filled with synchronicity, there are no accidents in these matters, and the cards that you get are the cards that are most useful for you to look at right now. These cards are the mirrors that most adequately reflect the circumstances of your question. This is the only sensible way to approach oracles. Otherwise, why bother digging out the cards at all. You could just sit and ruminate. The value in oracles is that they force us to extend our consciousness outside its normal patterns of thinking and look at matters from a new perspective. How does the "nine of swords" relate to my desire to open a yogurt bar? This is a new question that will result in new ways of understanding our circumstances and hopefully new and useful approaches to problems.

But do the cards predict the future? In themselves, no. Your reaction to the cards certainly does. If you get my beloved "nine of swords" and something inside you says, "yeah, I knew this wasn't going to work out," well, that informs you rather handily that you are heading in the wrong direction. There is a part of you that has already failed, and you either need to work with this part to change that, or you should give up. This part of you is leading you toward failure, and it will succeed if you don't address the issue. On the other hand, if you get this same card and immediately think," Hmm, my husband has been discouraging me about this the whole time, it's really making me miserable," then you have found another meaning for the card, and another matter that needs to be addressed. This is the power of the Tarot. It is a mirror.

The great danger in oracles in general, and Tarot in particular, is that if we aren't conscious of problems already, chances are we are trying to deny them. The symbols within any divinatory system other than a coin flip are subject to a great deal of creative interpretation, and we can miss the message entirely if we aren't watching for it vigilantly, or are more interested in simply deluding ourselves than seeing the message. There is a fearless, centered place that we must occupy in order to really perceive the correct message from any oracle. To get the most out of a Tarot reading we must really allow our intuition free rein to see what is going on within. But here is t he basic lay out of the spread. I will leave the rest to your wisdom and self-insight.

## The Hero's Journey Tarot Spread

THE FIRST CARD – "The Ordinary World" – This card represents the general current environment including things from the past that may be coloring present circumstances. This is an overview of what is happening "now."

THE SECOND CARD – "The Call to Adventure" – This represents the changing conditions that call you to action, the influences that directly demand your quest, or the forces hidden behind your quest.

THE THIRD CARD – "The Refusal of the Call" – This indicates the obstacles that stand in the way of your adventure. If it is a positive card it will represent something that while good, is not helpful to the situation at hand, or something you need to look at in a new way in regard to your quest.

THE FOURTH CARD - "Meeting with the Mentor" (supernatural aid) - This card may represent a helpful wise person, power or archetype that is reaching out to assist you as you begin. It can also represent the ideal that is being sought after, and that guides your path. Or it may indicate a challenge that must be overcome in order to receive help from the wise helper.

THE FIFTH CARD - "Crossing the First Threshold" - this card represents the energies and circumstances that will be meeting you as you first begin your quest. It is the basic circumstances of the road as you begin your adventure.

THE SIXTH CARD - "Tests, Allies or Enemies" (road of trials) as the name suggests, this will indicate friends, enemies or challenges that you will have to overcome or work with to get to your goal. The nature of these will be obvious in the card that comes up.

THE SEVENTH CARD "The Approach" This card indicates preparations that must be made in order to meet with the ordeal or great challenge of your quest. It may be skills you need to acquire or strengthen, or indicate weaknesses that need to be addressed.

THE EIGHTH CARD - "The Ordeal" - this represents the central challenge, the brink-of-death crisis that you will need to overcome in order to succeed. Your darkest hour, or greatest temptation to swerve from your path.

THE NINTH CARD - "The Reward" - this represents the immediate gain you will experience as you survive your ordeal. It may be some new knowledge or wisdom, or else some tangible reward.

THE TENTH CARD - "The Road Back" this card indicates the adventures experienced as you attempt to "return home" with your prize. The forces that would stop you or take back your reward. This may be the true darkest hour, or climax.

THE ELEVENTH CARD - "The Resurrection" this card represents the way in which you must transform in order to succeed. In order to conquer the forces against you, you must be reborn so to speak. This indicates the form of that resurrection.

THE TWELFTH CARD - "The Return with the Elixir" This card is the final outcome, the success or failure of your adventure. Is your story a comedy or a tragedy?

You may wish to study Vogler's *The Writer's Journey* and Campbell's *The Hero With a Thousand Faces* to gain a deeper understanding of these phases of your own personal adventures.

# Temporal Magick
## By Skott Holck

## Introduction

Among magicians and mystics there is a field of inquiry or study that is often ignored or not deeply contemplated. The reasons for this negligence are not easy to pin down; perhaps because of the inherent complexity, or due to the lack of any credible research into the field. Even among my own queries, both deliberate and accidental, I have been regarded as a deluded fool, a crackpot, someone who has lost touch with reality, a liar and a just plain freak. What field of magic could inspire such labels? I speak of time magick.

My own forays into this branch of study, which I have chosen to call Temporal Magick, began first as an accidental occurrence and then a deliberate response to the initial occurrence. Because of the nature of how my experience began, I find that I am often dismissed as someone who is simply responding to hallucination. I ask the reader to suspend judgment until I have completed my narrative, at which point whatever conclusions are arrived at are welcomed. I am sure that the opinions that are arrived at have been explored by myself, and I take no offense. I do not pretend to be an expert in the field, rather someone who has had a series of incidents that have guided an aspect of my life. The purpose of this and following essays will be to open the possibilities of what can be done with time magick as well as inviting others who have had similar experiences or who have worked with time magick to feel free to share their ideas and concepts.

Let me begin by stating that I had been ingesting LSD on a regular basis and considered myself a competent psychonaut. I had experienced the drug in a myriad of places and situations, I had tripped alone as well as with friends, I had experienced it outdoors and indoors, in public and private, I had seen movies and concerts under the influence; I felt completely prepared and had absolute certainty that I could handle whatever the chemical in concert with my mind could present to me. It seems that I was to be tested.

On this particular night, my wife and I consumed a dose of liquid LSD of uncertain micrograms. I noticed the effect of the chemical somewhat more rapidly than I was accustomed to and this inspired a slight twinge of nervousness. In order to relax into the experience and to prepare my mind, I selected an album and placed it in the stereo. I noticed the time on a digital clock as I pressed the play button. It was 7:14 pm. We lay back and began to enjoy the music as we began to enter into a psychedelic state. I was very familiar with the CD but for some reason the lyrics were coming across as rather stark and had a slight jarring quality to their meaning. I began to feel a slight twinge of anxiety. Though I knew every note and word to the album, it was feeling like I was hearing it for the first time. Though I could anticipate what came next, it was like a surprise. I was amused and confused at this and felt it was all part of the experience. As the album approached the halfway point I happened to glance at the clock again. It read 7:14. How could that be? I mulled this over for a few minutes as the music continued and the more I thought about it, the more unusual it seemed. I knew that in my current state odd perceptions were common place and that really this was nothing out of the ordinary. Surely my mind was playing tricks on me. I attempted to relate this to my wife but she did not really understand what I was trying to tell her; she was in her own world and having an experience of her own. I tried to ignore the clock, turning my back to it. I lit a cigarette and puffed away at it feeling the clock behind me. Nervously I glanced over my shoulder and the clock still displayed 7:14. I felt my heart rate begin to increase and a light sweat broke out on my face and along my hair line. I smoked and my breath felt shaky and ineffectual. I felt a slight tremor through my body and my anxiety increased. I tried to focus on the music hoping it would carry me to another place, another frame of mind. For a little while part of my enjoyed what I was hearing and it seemed that I was getting over the momentary bad spot. The music indeed brought me peace and serenity. Eventually the album came to an end and I wanted to hear more. I got up to change the CD, and there the clock sat with those green numbers, 7:14.

How could that be? I had listened to the full album and the clock had not ticked by a single minute. I thought to myself that my average acid trip lasted ten to twelve hours, if everything had experienced so far had taken less than a minute, how was I going to make it? Genuine panic set in. My heart beat jumped to an alarming rate and I could feel it thump in my chest. My knees buckled and I fell to the ground. I felt a tremendous spasm wrack my body and then suddenly there was blackness.

For a time, it seemed I had no awareness. I was in a state of oblivion. It could have been an eternity I drifted in this seeming nothingness, I will never know. It came to pass that at some point a small spark of sensation entered into whatever I was. There seemed to be some rudiment of thought, enough to make me wonder who I was, and how I came to be in the state I was in. I searched myself looking for memory, but really had nothing to draw upon. In this blackness I began to perceive a strange wavy sort of thing. I did not have a vocabulary to try to label what I encountered. I feel like I was aware of it, but I was without any of my typical senses. I feel I 'saw' it, but was not really in possession of the eyes with which to actually see. As I became more aware of what was before me, things began to focus. I perceived moments from a life, jumbled together and not really in any sort of order. It was like a life broken free of a chain of cause and effect. The memory bits seemed to be more in focus when there was strong emotional content to them. How I knew this, I cannot say, it just came to my mind that strong emotional memory was easier to experience. I then realized that this broken life before was none other than my own. The more I experienced it, the more certain I became that this was my life, jumbled as it was. I had by this point seen enough memories to realize that the state of mind I currently existed in was not normal. I felt that I needed to return to normal awareness. I felt that if I drifted too long in this 'in between' state, I might never return.

Knowing what I knew, gathered from little bits of my fragmented memory, I recalled that the last time I had been together, I had been feeling a strong emotion. It seemed logical that if I could become aware of the moment I had left myself, then I might be able to reintegrate and restore my shattered memory. I scanned this life before me, looking for an instant of intense emotion. It began to feel that it was of the utmost importance for me to get back to myself soon, before I slipped away forever. As this thought occurred to me, I saw an intense emotional period and felt this was what I was looking for. I grasped onto this point and felt myself slide into the memory.

I found myself standing on a porch in the back yard of a rural farmhouse. It was late at night and there was a vast array of stars overhead. I stared at them for a moment feeling very alone. My loneliness was deeper than I had ever thought possible. I could feel the stirring of others nearby, but their proximity did not alleviate the loneliness that assailed me. I realized that there was also profound sadness. This all was mixed with anger and fear. It was all held in some twisted check by a strong state of shock. I heard the voice of the paramedic in my mind repeating the words he had spoken a few moments ago, "I am afraid she has passed." I recalled the horror of administering CPR, wondering when the amb-ulance would arrive. They made it, but it had been too late, my efforts had been futile. My wife had died. I had indeed found a point of strong emotional content from my life but it did not seem to be the one I had been experiencing when I first left my body. I looked up at the stars realizing that I would never share this view with her again. Something told me that I was not supposed to be here and I once again faded to darkness.

When vision returned to me, I found myself laying on the floor tightly curled into the fetal position. I was shaking rather violently as if I was into a seizure. A moment later it passed and I was again in control of my faculties. My wife asked if I was okay. Lamely I said, "I don't know."

I sat up and my eyes caught sight of the clock which now read 7:15. I began to laugh uncontrollably, as only a person under the influence of LSD can laugh. It was a cathartic laugh and it somehow cleared my mind. For the rest of the trip, I was spent. I simply sat there as the world passed around my. My mind felt a little like a caldera after a volcano had erupted. A deep change had occurred and I did not know how to deal with it. I longed to return to normal headspace and peace of mind. The dawn could not come soon enough.

The next day came naturally but I was in no way back to normal. I was still very much troubled by what I had experienced. The music that had been playing continued to run through my mind, over and over again. It was as if the audio experience had been left on some permanent playback. Try as I might I could not make it stop. Fortunately, I liked the album or perhaps things might have been different. I also began to have recurring images of the stars I had seen from the porch, as well as the sadness and shock I had experienced. As the days passed I would find myself waking up with a feeling that she had died, and that I was alone. I would panic for a moment until I discovered that she was alive and that she was next to me. I was being haunted by something that had not occurred.

It began to worsen. One morning I awoke and was again standing on that porch looking at the stars. My mind went back over the experience of administering CPR, and my attempt to keep her alive failing. I recalled all the visits to the doctor, especially the angiogram she had just had done earlier that day. I thought of the first heart attack she had four months ago, and how terrifying those months had been. I wondered about whether or not our move had been the wisest of choices. Had the stress of our last year been too much for her? Did my need to write my book contribute to her death? These thoughts filled my mind as I groggily awoke to my normal life. It seemed I was having more memories of things that had not come to pass. It seemed that in that brief moment when I had stood on that porch, my mind was full of memories, but since that night of her passing had not occurred yet, I was having memories of things that had not occurred yet.

I could not bring myself to tell her about what had happened. It seemed too weird to think about. How do you tell a person you remember them dying? I kept it inside and tried not to think about it. This was not an easy task. Each time I awoke with the feeling of standing on the porch, it seemed there was more in my mind. I was remembering more of my past. This resulted in more memories of things to come from the perspective of my day to day life. I felt like I was losing my mind and the isolation was becoming agony. The more time that passed, the more difficult it was talk about it, and the more memories I seemed to have. It became so difficult to deal with, I began to miss work, and ignore my friends. I felt like I had gone crazy and that there would be no way to get better.

I tried to take control the best way I could think of. I began to perform banishing rituals several times a day in an effort to gain stability. I began to meditate frequently in an effort to still my mind and find peace. I tried to do research trying to find someone else with similar experiences, but what brief accounts I came across read like the ramblings of madmen. So much of my efforts were going in to maintaining myself, that I began to loose touch with the world around me. For a time my friends stopped coming around as I was likely to be noncommunicative. I ended up losing my job due to the fact that I missed work so much and that when I was there, I was not effective. It got worse and worse. More and more memories began to intrude upon me, and each time I gained memories of things to come, my grip on reality slipped.

I had been a fairly serious student of the occult for several years at this point in my life and was well read on the subject for a novice. I ran an informal Qabalah study group, and I was meditating daily. I felt that at some point I would get down to serious work and go about the necessary steps to achieve what Aleister Crowley called the Knowledge and Conversation with my Holy Guardian Angel. My magical studies felt like the one arena of my life that had a semblance of stability. When I was working magick, I felt like I was in control. It dawned on me that I needed to apply my magick work to my life in general, and this might lead to an overall stability. I was not sure what I needed to do, only that I needed to do something.

As the months wore on I continued to have more and more memories of things to come. I began to even piece things together into a loose sequence. I became aware that the memory of my wife dying was five years from this point. I saw many things that would come to pass, some of them good and some of them not. My recollection of events to come was in no way complete. It seemed there was still plenty of room to move through my life without feeling bound to a deterministic path. And yet, despite my choices, things I remembered had a way of coming to pass despite my efforts to do something different. Knowing that I had five years of this sort of living was daunting to me. I refused to tell my wife about it; it just seemed so unbelievable and that perhaps if I did not mention it, it might not happen. She obviously knew something was wrong with me as I seemed to have had a breakdown of sorts. I had grown afraid of emotion and was living like a robot, trying not to give in to my feelings. More memories came and the task of maintaining was becoming more and more difficult.

One afternoon I was thinking about what had occurred to me, and I was going over the weird events of my life. I was thinking about the time I had floated in the oblivion-like state and then had witnessed my life as a series of emotional responses. Since I had looked into my life and saw such an emotional response from a point in the future, then on some level, my live was already lived. From the perspective outside of the time flow, all lives had already been lived. All events of the universe had occurred. Outside of time, everything that happened in the universe had already done so. From the initial stirring of pre-atomic energy and matter to whatever the end was, outside of time it had all happened. For me this line of thinking was a comfort. I realized that in five years my wife was going to die, it would be the end her existence on this one level, but beyond that, I realized that I would go on. There was life for me after this event. I would get through it and go on. I figured that since I was devoting so much energy to my magical studies and the bettering of myself, then at some point in my future, I would be wiser and more spiritually evolved. This future self would know what I had done to make it through the difficulties I had faced. It dawned on me that my idea of a Holy Guardian Angel was a being essentially myself but at a point where I had achieved enlightenment. If I had glimpsed my life from a perspective outside of time once, then why could I not do it again? I began to devote my energy to just that.

My meditation was of a directed sort at this point. I was not simply trying to still the mind and quiet thought, I was willfully trying to force myself out of my body so that I might once again glimpse my life laid out before me and from that point discover myself in a more evolved state. For weeks I worked at this and had no success. I feared that I was deluding myself and that I had really lost touch with reality. When I was not meditating, I was reading books on quantum mechanics looking for a scientific justification of what I was attempting to do. The crisis of my life intensified and I approached a breaking point.

One evening I lay back on the floor after I had finished meditating. I had done a fairly good job at clearing my mind but had not achieved what I had intended. I was frustrated and lay there thinking that I might never bring myself to a place where I could cope with my predicament. I sort of drifted into a state not unlike one feels before sleep. I was aware of the room around me, but there was a sudden change. In the dimness I noticed a figure emerge from the shadows. At first the figure was a silhouette standing in the corner. My heart rate increased slightly but I did not feel threatened. I sat up and the figure emerged from the shadow stepping toward me. I then saw the figure in ever growing detail. It was something like looking into a mirror, but different at the same time. The figure before me had my face but it was marked by age. Where I had long hair, this person was bald. Its eyes were paler than mine and it sort of hunched over bit. I realized that I was looking at myself as an old man. I was too shocked to speak. I just stared not sure what was going to happen. I thought to myself that now was my opportunity to get guidance about how to deal with what was going on in my life. The figure stepped forward and placed a hand upon my head. The contact was soothing, with a weird etheric warmth. There was solidity too it, but not quite the same as with tangible matter.

He held his hand on my head for a moment and then said, "Open your heart, Andonkis."

He broke contact, turned and walked into the shadow, disappearing. I blinked a few times trying to make sense of what had occurred. Not wanting to forget the moment, I grabbed a scrap of paper and jotted down the words he had said to me.

I spent the next few months trying to make sense of everything. It seemed clear that after my experience at having memories for things that had not occurred yet, I had shut down. I was trying hard not to feel. Living had become a routine that wished I could escape from. I knew that in less than five years, Carrie was going to die, and I had been trying to hide from the pain of that knowledge. I had disconnected myself from emotion and I was essentially awaiting the inevitable. But now, after deliberately trying to reach myself in the future, I had a single simple message. I was to open my heart.

This message did not immediately restore my life to what it had been. In fact it was only a very small tool in which to help me live my life. No longer would I let fear of pain keep me from living. I accepted the fact that in the not too distant future, Carrie was going to die, but then so were we all. I could deal with that fact just as I could deal with anything. All I needed to do was to open my heart and let myself feel whatever came. The word 'Andonkis' became my magical name, one that I still use to this day. I delved into its meaning and found many truths unsuitable to discuss in this exposition at this time.

As the years passed I found an unforeseen gift arise from the experience. I 'remembered' a novel I had written, as well as all the steps necessary to get it done. My life was a little like living in a book that you had read years ago; some of the details were lost, but you still remember the main parts. When I sat to write the novel, it was more like I was recalling it. It came naturally and seemed to write itself. The novel was about a man slipping out of time.

Inevitably the time came when I had to face the night that Carrie died. It was a weird day. She had suffered a minor heart attack a few months prior and she was undergoing tests to see how her condition was progressing. We returned to the farmhouse we were living at and I knew what was coming. It seemed in a strange way, she was aware of it also. She moved about our place spending time with me and the cats, letting herself have a few hours of simple peace. Late that night she went into cardiac arrest. I found myself standing on the porch looking up at the stars. My experience had come full circle, and for the first time in five years, I had memories of only things in the past.

It is now over twelve years since Carrie had passed away and in those years I have given much thought and reflection to what had happened to me. I had lived for a time with memories that I should not have had. For that time I was remembering the future. It seems that with what I have experienced, there is a vast possibility that could be explored using my experience as a basis. I wonder if there will come a time when I, as an old man will need to travel back to my younger self to offer a kernel of advice so that I will be able to deal with memories dislodged from their proper time. That makes me wonder how much a person could improve by offering and receiving advice from their own future self. It can certainly boggle the mind.

# Advanced Magick for Beginners

A book review by Giles Vint

*Advanced Magick for Beginners*
*By Alan Chapman*
*Published by Aeon Books*
*176 pages*
*ISBN: 978-1904658412*

*Advanced Magick for Beginners* by Alan Chapman is quite possibly one of the most important books on magick ever published. For in it, the Author gives what in my opinion is the best explanation as to how magick works. Many have tried to explain this, but no one has truly succeeded. They either didn't quite get it, or their attempts weren't really that clear. Here Mr. Chapman succeeds in providing the simplest and clearest explanation to date. We're given a six-step process whereby any act or form of magick, including divination, can be performed successfully. He shows that magick is so simple that everyone overlooks the fact that they have the ability to manipulate reality.

The basic idea of the book can be summarized in Chapman's definition of magick, "Magick is the art, science and culture of experiencing truth." His basic six-step instruction in the performance of magick is a revolution in simplicity:

1. Decide what you want to occur.

2. Ensure that what you want to occur has a means of manifestation.

3. Choose an experience.

4. Decide that the experience means the same thing as what you want to occur.

5. Perform the act/undergo the experience.

6. Result.

It is often said that to work magick effectively you have to do this, or you have to do that. Magical laws such as sympathy, the magical link, altered states of consciousness, and forgetting the statement of desire, etc. are shown to be completely unnecessary, although quite useful if you wish to employ them as magical techniques. The reader will be able to take this further and see through many other ideas and rules that have apparently been set in stone. Techniques from other books and systems will be made so much more useable and effective, and it will become abundantly clear how they work. This includes the classical Grimoires, and traditional sources such as Agrippa.

The book is written in a straight to the point manner, and covers all aspects and techniques of western magick, plus several other things beside. Numerous exercises are given throughout, so that the reader can prove to himself the effectiveness of the techniques and subjects he's reading about. Plus it forms a curriculum that anyone at any level of skill and knowledge can use, on it's own or with other curriculums. Everyone should read this book, whatever system(s) you use, whether you're a Beginner, or an Adept. Even though I've been studying and practicing magick for more than seventeen years, I found things in things in this book that caused me to have repeated Aha! moments. All techniques discussed are linked back to the six step process to show how they work. Although the style is what some may call "freestyle," this book goes far beyond what Chaos Magick had to offer. Plus it brings back into play several babies that the Chaotes threw out with the bath water.

While reading, I thought I understood how the six steps worked, and therefore magick. But it wasn't until I was almost at the end of the book that I read something which blew me away, and I finally got it. So you must finish the book to glean all it has to offer. Then read it again.

You can order a copy from Amazon or another online bookseller, or directly from the publisher at: www.aeonbooks.co.uk

For further material by Alan Chapman and his colleague Duncan Barford, check out their website at www.thebaptistshead.co.uk which also includes some interesting podcasts. I also highly recommend their book *Blood of the Saints*, which is a digest of much of the material on the website, for those who prefer to hold a book in their hand rather than reading from a screen

# The Thule Conspiracy
## Part Two
### By Jason Augustus Newcomb

## Chapter 2

Too much, these dreams were too much. They were getting more and more frequent, and each one seemed more grisly than the last. Meg turned to see if she had disturbed Michael's sleep. He gazed up at her sleepily.

"Another bad dream?" asked Michael with his crooked smile. She loved that smile, but it was a cold solace this morning.

"Yeah," she muttered, slipping off the side of the bed. She was still naked from last night's debauch. The sweat that covered her made her feel chilled. And despite the fact that they had been sleeping together for over a year, Meg still felt a bit uncomfortable letting Michael look at her fully naked in the daylight. It wasn't because she felt unattractive. She knew she had a sexy body. She stood nearly five feet nine, with a slender waist and sensuously round hips. She knew she was beautiful. She did feel a bit uncomfortable about her breasts. They were rather full, and even at twenty-six they weren't as firm and perky as they had been in her teens. But that really wasn't what made her uncomfortable. It was the very nature of the intimacy itself.

She scooped up her camisole and panties, slipping them on as casually as possible. She was in too deep. It was all becoming too normal, too suburban. And she knew she wasn't normal. Could she ever be normal? The nightmares were just the tip of the iceberg, the only part she allowed herself to share. Michael could never understand it all. He was a professor of European literature. What could he know about the things she saw, the things she experienced? And could she even dare to find out? She wasn't even sure where this relationship was going anymore.

Meg looked over at the little digital radio alarm clock on the bedside table: 5:23 AM. It was too early. "You can go back to sleep, sweetie," she said, trying to sound calm as she sat back down on the edge of the bed. "Caitlin won't be up for another hour or so."

Michael's little daughter Caitlin was the most adorable creature Meg had ever known. She turned five shortly after Meg and Michael met, and Caitlin was already practically thinking of Meg as her new mommy. But Meg wasn't at all sure that was what Michael was thinking. Could Meg ever even be a proper mother to anyone? Everything seemed to be spinning out of her control.

Michael had picked Meg up at the restaurant where she worked as a waitress. He wasn't the first guy she had gone home with, though she never mentioned that to him. It was all playing the nice, good girl with Michael. And she was a good girl, most of the time at least. She had never cheated on Michael, never even considered it, though she certainly had offers nearly every night. But they were all boys, silly boys, even the dirty old men were just silly boys.

Michael was a real man. She knew that the moment she saw him. He was so calm and good-natured, he never really even hit on her at all in the restaurant. He and Caitlin were eating at the restaurant twice a week back then, Wednesdays and Fridays, and more often than not they sat in her section. Caitlin requested Meg to be their waitress every time. Meg thought Michael was a good looking guy the first time she saw him, but Meg spent so much time giving attention to Caitlin that she hardly spoke to Michael for weeks. When he finally got around to asking her out, he even did it through his daughter Caitlin. She still remembered it vividly, 'Caitlin was wondering if you'd like to eat dinner with us sometime, rather than just serving it to us.' It was such a strange request that she wasn't even sure if it was a romantic date at first. But that night in his bed, after Caitlin was fast asleep, the matter was more than cleared up.

Right here in this same bed, the one she'd slept in nearly every night since. Michael was the most charming and intelligent man she'd ever met. He was nearly ten years older than she was, but that was such a good thing. There were no childish scenes or possessive jealousy. Michael was a grown up, self assured and comfortable with himself. She loved him with every part of her being, and she loved Caitlin just as much. She was in too deep.

Michael was a widower, his wife died very suddenly from a tumor in her brain before Caitlin was even two. Meg had known Caitlin practically as long as Caitlin had known her real mother. Meg was in way too deep.

Tears began to well in Meg's eyes. She wasn't sure if it was because of the dream or just because of every-thing. Things had been a bit strained lately. The subject of marriage came up again last week. Had she brought it up? Why would she have brought it up? She couldn't even remember how it started. It must have been something about Caitlin. But Michael had ended it. He ended it with just a look, just the briefest expression that slipped across his face. It was just the faintest quiver of dread. That look left her feeling like nothing but a whore to him.

In a way she kind of understood. Michael came from a fairly conservative Jewish family, not orthodox or anything, but fairly Jewish nonetheless. Michael wasn't observant at all, but his mother was deeply involved with synagogue, keeping kosher, the community, Shabbat, the whole thing. She always looked at Meg like she was a whore, but that never bothered her as long as Michael loved her. But in that brief glance from Michael Meg felt like she'd never be more than the 'Goyish slut' that Michael kept for his amusement until he found a nice Jewish girl to really settle down with again.

Meg wiped the tears from her eyes, hoping Michael wasn't watching. Unfortunately he was.

"You crying, sweetie?" he said, his voice still heavy and raspy from sleep.

"No," she said, then corrected herself. "Well, just a little." She tried to smile.

"You want to talk about it?" he asked in his warm, wonderful, understanding tone.

She turned to him. She wanted to talk to him. She wanted to tell him everything. The dream, the violence, the dead with their cold fingers, the skull, that horrible skull! She wanted to tell him about all her visions, how she just knew things sometimes. So much worse than déjà vu, she felt like space and time rolled back and forth on top of her, like she was sometimes drowning in the ocean of her own life experiences, without any order or sequence. She wanted to tell him how he had hurt her, how she had never loved anyone like she loved him, how she loved Caitlin just the same. But somehow only, "Not really," slipped out, and she turned away.

"'kay," he said, rolling up on his elbow. He stared at her back for a while. "Is it still that... that Nazi stuff?" he asked, his nose wrinkling involuntarily, his lips quivering into a frown.

She didn't see it, but she still regretted ever mentioning anything about those dreams. Maybe that was why he would never think about marrying her. She dreamed about Nazis! Why did she ever tell her Jewish boyfriend that she dreamed about Nazis? How stupid can you get? Why did she even bother thinking, fantasizing, that she could marry anyone? She was a crazy person. This life she was leading, it was all a masquerade. Underneath it all she was completely insane. She knew that with perfect clarity. She was in too deep.

Meg stood up and found her purse where she'd tossed it on the floor last night. She burrowed her fingers past wads of waitressing cash and found what she was looking for. She pulled out a cigarette and a lighter. She pressed the cigarette between her lips.

"Aren't we quitting?" said Michael, sitting up and throwing his legs over the side of the bed.

Meg shot him a cool glare and lit the cigarette. She turned away.

Michael didn't know what to make of Meg anymore. It had all seemed so perfect at first. Meg was by far the most beautiful woman that he'd ever been with. Smart too, and funny. Sometimes she got a bit quiet, sullen, but that was just a mysterious box that he thought he would someday figure out how to open. The mystery had been part of her allure. Here was a girl who graduated Magna cum Laude from D.C.U. with a degree in neurobiology, and she was working as a waitress in a diner. It was fascinating at first, but now it was just getting frustrating.

Michael didn't know what to do. Caitlin adored her, worshipped her. She'd even called her mommy a few times, though she stopped when she saw that it made him nervous. Children are so observant, so much wiser than adults are sometimes. And Caitlin loved Meg completely.

Michael loved Meg too. He knew that. He loved her so much. Perhaps even more than he'd ever loved Rachel, his wife, though he rarely allowed himself to think about that at all. His marriage to Rachel, it was so short. He had been thirty-one and his mother put so much pressure on him to settle down. Rachel was just what she wanted, the right family, the right religion, the right everything for his mother. But was she ever right for Michael? There had never been enough time to find out. Was Meg somehow more right? Was she what he really wanted? Was this gorgeous blonde mess his dream girl?

Meg threw on a silky pink robe, a sexy little robe Michael gave her a few months ago, and strutted off toward the kitchen. Michael got up, threw on some underwear and a t-shirt, and followed her.


Meg sat at the thick, oak kitchen table, staring at the cabinets, trying not to think about anything at all. She concentrated on her cigarette, feeling the smoke in her lungs, that raspy swollen feeling somewhere between pleasure and pain. That was enough.

Michael shoved a glass of orange juice in front of her, and she took it. She stared at it for a while before she bothered to take a sip. She didn't even notice the taste of it.

"I just don't know what to do with myself anymore," she said without any inflection.

Michael didn't really know how to respond. "I wish you'd let me in on it," he said finally.

"Do you?" Meg looked up at him, her gaze impenetrable. She shook her head. "I don't think you could understand."

Down the hall from the kitchen, a door opened, and Caitlin Lieberman poked her head around. She heard her Daddy and Meg talking, first in their bedroom, now in the kitchen. She knew they were up. She'd been having one of her secret early morning tea parties with her dolls, but she was still hungry for some real breakfast. She was glad they were awake. But were they having grown up time? Her little hand held the door tightly, the edge of her pink pony pajamas just barely visible.

"You never let me try to understand," she heard her Daddy say. It sure sounded like grown up time to Caitlin, but she was too curious and hungry to stay in her room. She crept down the hall into the kitchen. There she saw Meg slumped at the table, looking really sad. She hated it when Meg was sad. She hoped it wasn't anything she'd done. Or even worse, she hoped it wasn't something that Daddy had done. She didn't like it when they were fighting. She knew they weren't married, and that Meg could still go away forever. There had been a few others, a few other women that Daddy brought home. They all left and she never saw them again. She never liked them as much as she liked Meg, but that didn't mean that Meg wouldn't go away. Daddy had to be nice to Meg. She didn't want Meg to ever go away.

"What's wrong, Meg?" asked Caitlin.

Meg looked down at Caitlin, surprised to see her right there in front of her. Meg smiled at Caitlin warmly, wiping her eyes. Caitlin always made her feel better about things. She tossed her cigarette into the half drunk orange juice and scooped up Caitlin onto her lap.

"Hi, cutie. What are you doing up so early?"

"Nothing," said Caitlin guiltily. She never told anyone about her secret tea parties. They were just for her and her dolls. "Why are you sad?" she asked, changing the subject back to Meg.

"Meg's okay Caitlin," said Michael. "She just had a bad dream. That's all."

"Oh," said Caitlin precociously. "Don't be sad, Meg. I sometimes have bad dreams too. It's just dreams. They can't hurt you. Not really." She smiled at Meg brightly.

Meg squeezed Caitlin against her chest. "Thank you, cutie. That makes me feel a lot better." She did really feel better. Caitlin's warm little body melted away everything.

"You smell like smoke, Meg," said Caitlin. She drew her face up into a scolding frown.

"Oh yeah?" said Meg, smiling and sniffing. "Well, you smell like peanut butter."

"What?" said Caitlin, feigning complete ignorance. "Why would I smell like peanut butter?"

"Have you been sneaking midnight snacks?" asked Michael, smiling.

"Me?" asked Caitlin. "No." It was true. She had only eaten peanut butter crackers with her dolls around sunrise.

"We'll both have to get washed up before we take you to school," said Meg merrily. Neither Meg nor Michael cared to inquire further into Caitlin's peanut butter enigma. All the stress was completely gone. That was enough. Domestic bliss was once again established. At least for the moment.

## Chapter 3

With Caitlin safely deposited at school, Michael and Meg made their way to their favorite coffee shop, where they often shared a cup or two before Michael had to get to the university. The drive was a bit quiet, but little more than usual. They often sat together quietly, just silently enjoying each other's company.

When they arrived at the coffee shop they got their Styrofoam cups of coffee from the counter and sat down together at a pink and gray plastic booth. They sat right next to each other, facing the counter, just like they always did. That way they could 'people watch' toge-ther. Michael rested his hand on Meg's thigh and Meg intertwined her fingers over his hand. It felt good. Both of them felt better. An endless stream of morning commuters came and went, hot morning beverages in hand.

"What do you think would happen if they outlawed coffee?" asked Michael lightly.

"Western civilization would grind to a screeching halt," said Meg with a smirk.

"I think you're right."

"Until the Mafia stepped in," giggled Meg.

"Right, there'd be Cappuccino Speak Easys all over the place." They both laughed.

A large television hung above the counter, broadcasting the local news loudly. The report caught Meg's attention.

"Adding to the staggering rise in hate motivated crimes in D.C. Metropolitan area over the last few weeks comes this latest tragedy which has shocked investigators and reporters alike," said the anchorman, a gray-haired fellow whose stretched features appeared to have undergone a significant amount of cosmetic surgery. "In what can only be called an outrageous attack on the Jewish community, early this morning Joshua Cohen..."

Meg's face went white as a photo of the young man she'd just dreamed about was blazoned across the screen. He looked happy, perhaps a year or so younger than when she'd seen hm, wearing a suit instead of merely his underwear, but the face was unmistakable. Meg tried to keep her focus on the story, but she felt faint, like the world was spinning up around her.

"...a young executive at National Bank here in Washington was apparently taken from his home by unknown assailants. Signs of forced entry, racist and Nazi graffiti spray-painted inside his home have led police to believe an abduction the only likely scenario. Cohen's whereabouts are still unknown at this hour. Police are searching for witnesses..."

This wasn't the first time. Other dreams had really happened. Others turned out to be true. But this was the worst time. Her head swam. She felt like she was floating up out of herself. This wasn't the worst dream she'd ever had, but it was the most horrible dream she'd ever had that was actually becoming reality before her. She only hoped that not all of the horrors she had experienced in dreams were really true. It was all too much to bear.

She stood up swiftly, leaning on Michael's shoulder. It was too quick. Stars swam before her eyes, "Oh my God," she muttered as everything faded swiftly into blackness. She felt herself falling, fainting. Cold dead hands caught her as she fell, easing her into the dark emptiness.

When she regained consciousness she found herself lying on the floor, with Michael cradling her head in his arms.

"Meg? Are you okay?" he asked as he gazed down at her with deep concern. "Did you hit your head?"

"No, uh," It only took a moment for her to remember what was happening. "Oh my God!" she said again, scrambling to her feet. Without another word she ran out of the coffee shop onto the street.

Michael stumbled after her. By the time he caught up with her she was standing by the car, and he was gasping for breath. "What the hell, Meg? What are you doing?" He reached out and took hold of her arm, as if she might take off unexpectedly again.

"Michael..." said Meg, unsure what she could say. Telling him would just alienate him even more, but she couldn't just say nothing, not now. "That story... that was my dream."

"What?" Michael couldn't comprehend what she was trying to say.

"I know you're not going to believe me," she said, tears bursting forth. She shoved his hand off her arm and turned away. "That was my dream, the dream this morning. The one that made me scream."

"What, the news story in there?"

Meg covered her eyes with her hands. "Yes," she cried out, sobbing. "I saw that guy. I saw the guys who took him. Skinheads. I saw them, I saw their faces. I saw their car. I saw them kill him, I saw everything!" She wept loudly, unaware and unconcerned about the people staring as they passed by.

Michael tried to ignore them too. He put his hand on her shoulder, gently soothing her. He couldn't believe she really thought she'd had some sort of psychic dream. What a strange thing to think. He wanted to calm her down, to somehow reassure her that this was nothing to be concerned about. "Now Meg, I know these nightmares upset you-"

Meg threw his hand off her shoulder and spun to him. "Damn it, Michael!" She knew he wouldn't believe her. He was always so logical, so complacent in his intellectual atheist, materialist blindfold. "Give me the god damned car keys!"

Something in her voice made it impossible to resist the command. He fumbled around in his pockets. Still, he couldn't help but ask, "Are you sure you'll be okay to drive?"

The drive was unbearable. The twosome argued the whole way downtown to the university. Meg felt that she was obligated to go to the police and tell them what she saw, Michael insisted that the idea was crazy. Meg shouted quite a lot. Michael tried to remain calm. About halfway there an old man stepped out in front of the moving car and Meg laid down so hard on the horn that Michael thought the guy was going to have a heart attack. But still Michael couldn't bring himself to believe her story.

"It's just not possible, Meg."

"I know it's not possible, but it's true."

"You can't go to the police and tell them that you witnessed a crime in a dream." Michael scowled. "It's ridiculous."

"I have to. I'm an eyewitness. The only witness."

They pulled into the university campus and drove up the grassy tree-lined lane. Michael knew he only had another minute or two to talk sense into Meg before she would be free to follow whatever absurd path she wanted.

"Please, Meg, I'm begging you not to make a fool of yourself. I don't know what's motivating this. I just don't get it."

"I've had some kind of fucking paranormal experience. That's what's motivating this," shrieked Meg. Her face was red and blotchy.

"There's no such thing as fucking paranormal experiences," said Michael, raising his own voice.

Meg sighed. Tears streamed down her face. "I know," she said. "But that doesn't change the fact that I've had one." She didn't bother to mention the many other experiences she had. It didn't matter anyway.

Meg pulled the car over to the sidewalk where Michael always got out. She turned off the engine. She stared straight ahead, breathing raggedly. She wouldn't look at Michael. She couldn't.

"Look, I've gotta go." Said Michael. He was afraid to get out of the car, but he had to be in class in less than ten minutes. "We'll talk about this later, I promise. We'll figure it out. Just please don't go to the police."

"Fine," said Meg, sighing heavily. She still wouldn't look him in the eyes.

"Okay, I love you babe." Michael kissed his fingers and touched them to her reddened cheeks.

"Love you," she said hollowly. As Michael walked toward the brick buildings Meg turned the car around. She dug out her cell phone and got online to find directions to the nearest police station.

*To be continued…*

# SPECIAL SUPPLEMENT:
# The Bavarian Illuminati
## In Their Own Words
## By Jason Augustus Newcomb

There has been an enormous amount of speculation about the Bavarian Illuminati, virtually since its inception in 1776 and rather quick demise in the 1780s. It has been the cornerstone of numerous conspiracy theories, probably gaining a height of popularity with Robert Anton Wilson and Robert Shea's *Illuminatus Trilogy*. "Illuminati" has become a standard generic term to refer to whatever dark cabal you suspect of pulling the strings behind the scenes in society and government.

I became briefly interested in the historical Illuminati when I first read the above satirical story, but I quickly lost my enthusiasm when I saw the incredible mire of opposing and nonsensical misinformation out there. As Wilson might put it with tongue in cheek (if he wasn't presently hanging out with Wilhelm Reich), "The disinformation put out there by the Illuminati so that no one will notice what they're really up to."

In fact, a good deal of popular mythology about the Illuminati actually seems to have been created or at least popularized by Wilson and Shea themselves. For instance the bit about the obverse side of the seal of United States. You know the one. The eye in the triangle above the truncated pyramid. Well, I hate to disappoint would-be Illuminists out there who have tattooed that symbol on themselves or some such, but that symbol has absolutely nothing to do with the Bavarian Illuminati whatsoever. Adam Weishaupt's Illuminati did not use the symbol, or anything like it. It was not mysteriously handed off to Jefferson or some other founding father in the dark hours of the night. In fact, it was created by a congressional committee. If you look around on the internet you can find all sorts of variants and other suggestions that various members of the committee vied for. The basic "eye in triangle" of the design can actually be found in quite a lot of Catholic churches (and some occult orders). It is a fairly common motif to present the "all-seeing" eye of God, or "providence" as the secular humanist founding fathers preferred, as an eye in a triangle. The triangle is most likely an allusion to the trinity, and thus it is ultimately rather Christian icon-ography.

And as far as Wilson and Shea's fairly tall tale about Adam Weishaupt and George Washington being the same person, well take a look at any drawings or paintings of either of them and you will see that Wilson and Shea clearly needed some stronger corrective lenses.

The peculiar thing about the Illuminati myth is that both right wing and left wing conspiracy theorists like to cast the Illuminati as the villains in their psychodramas. The right wingers think they are a bunch of communist Satanists hell bent on destroying the moral and social order. The left wingers think they are a bunch of rich bankers and old money bent on enslaving the common man. Both are certain they are everywhere, and that media and politics are largely controlled by them. It is

such a mass of incoherent, reactionary, paranoid ramblings that any sane person would run from it.

But I am clearly not that sane, and my curiosity was
once again awakened a couple of years ago after seeing
John Michael Greer give a lecture in which he suggested
that the Bavarian Illuminati was in fact a very small and
fairly unsuccessful little fraternity. Somehow the idea of
it being a failure struck my interest much more than the
idea of it being a giant world-devouring cabal. A group
that never amounted to much of anything, yet somehow
managed to get cast as the world's great villain. How
intriguing, how did something like that happen?

Well, it seems like the truth is probably somewhat
more in the middle. The Illuminati did spread throughout Germany and even a bit further. The Illuminati did
have several thousand members at its height. It did take
over and influence a great deal of early German
freemasonry. It did have some rather clever and sneaky
methods of influencing and enticing members. And
Weishaupt did attempt to influence governments in a
revolutionary way, though the extent of his success is
hard to ascertain. The ideals and philosophy of the
"Enlightenment Era" were spreading quite well on their
own and it's impossible to say how much influence
secret societies played in transformative events like the
French Revolution. Certainly the world that we presently live in bears little resemblance to the vision of Adam
Weishaupt, at least as it is presented in the writings we
have available.

And it is to these writings that I want to devote this
special supplement. I have placed it as a special supplement because it is rather long and may seem boring if
you are not interested in the subject. I have ghettoized it
to spare you. So by all means put this book down and

consider it done if you are not at all interested in the Bavarian Illuminati.

But since the movie *Angels and Demons,* based on the Dan Brown (of daVinci Code fame) novel of the same title, will soon fill the world with even more spurious nonsense about the Illuminati, I thought a presentation of this material would be timely.

There have been numerous books written about the Illuminati, going all the way back to the 1780s. Most of them are either viciously polemical or simply salacious conspiracy fodder. Strangely, a huge amount of actual Bavarian Illuminati materials, rituals, philosophy, codes of conduct and other odds and ends exist. They were published by the Bavarian Government in the 1780s, and Weishaupt published numerous explanations and apologia for the rest of his life. However, all of this was in German, and little has ever been available in English.

One of the few English sources of original Illuminati source material available is in Abbé Barreul's *Memoirs Illustrating the History of Jacobinism, Part Three,* published 1798. This is an almost contemporary account of the Illuminati, and he quotes from the actual source materials extensively. However, most of his quotes are contextualized amidst his highly critical, insulting and defamatory text. He regularly calls Weishaupt a "villain" and a "monster," throughout the work, and it almost seems funny sometimes when you read what he is calling monstrous such as, "Liberty and Equality are the essential rights that man in his original and primitive perfection received from nature." How monstrous! What would happen to our precious Kings and Princes if such vile and evil ideas spread! I mean this seems like pretty tame stuff by today's standards. In comparison with other bogies like the Branch Davidians, Charles Manson, The Nazis, The Moonies, Scientologists, and the many hundreds of other little personality cults that have caught the world's attention, the Bavarian Illuminati seem like a comparatively harmless bunch.

So, I thought I would put together the bulk of this quoted material from Barreul, without comment, so that it can be viewed on its own terms. I am in no way trying to defend or laud the Illuminati, as they do seem to have engaged in some shady and manipulative behavior. But it seems that you don't get world renowned without a bit of shady behavior. Nearly all of history's famous groups, gurus, cults and religions have used similar tactics, and most much more successfully.

It should be kept in mind that this material was chosen by Abbé Barreul to suit his purpose of attacking the Illuminati. This is the material he felt would be most damning. For the most part he looks a fool in his condemnation, as many of the ideals of the illuminati are the ideals of the American Revolution as well. Of course Weishaupt went much further, desiring to rid the world not only of tyrants and kings, but also personal property. Still, it all seems far milder without Barreul's vicious commentary, but there may be quite a bit more material out there in German that could paint an even more benevolent image of the fraternity. I really don't know. It should also be kept in mind that this material is double translated, that is from German to French, French to English, so there may be a bit of corruption. But Barreul was considered a competent scholar in his day, so the translations are probably not too distorted. However, he does not always clearly distinguish whether a quote is directly from Weishaupt or one of his companions, so I won't try to make that distinction much either. It is also sometimes a bit difficult to be certain what is an "actual quote," and what is a "speculative quote" crafted by Barruel to fill in details.

Some of these quotes seem a bit too self-indicting for me to entirely accept them.

But before we move on to the writings themselves, for reference here is an approximation of the hierarchy of the Bavarian Illuminati. It is a bit of a confused matter, as the names and degrees shifted over time and in different circumstances. This is a very general view:

Student
Novice
Minerval
Minor Illuminee
Major Illuminee (or Scotch Novice)
Scotch Knight
Epopt (or priest)
Regent (or Prince)
Magus (or Mage)
Rex (or Man King)

There are a few other variations, and the rites of freemasonry were apparently often thrown in there before Illuminee, but that is a basic view.

Some of the following quotes may seem rather out of context, or out of the blue, but it is even more out of context surrounded by Barreul's vitriol. But I think you will see that none of the myths about the Illuminati adequately represent the reality at all. I have broadly separated them into a few categories, though some quotes could certainly fit in more than one category. So, let's take a look at what the Illuminati was all about, in their own words.

## The Goals and Philosophy of the Illuminati

"Liberty and Equality are the essential rights that man in his original and primitive perfection received from nature. Property struck the first blow at Equality; political Society, or Governments, were the first oppressors of Liberty; the supporters of Governments and property are the religious and civil laws; therefore, to reinstate man in his primitive rights of Equality and Liberty, we must begin by destroying all Religion, all civil society, and finish by the destruction of all property."

"Yes, princes and nations shall disappear from off the face of the earth; yes, a time shall come when man shall acknowledge no other law but the great book of nature: This revolution shall be the work of the secret societies, and that is one of our grand mysteries."

"Let the laughers laugh, let the scoffers scoff; he that compares the past with the present, will see that nature continues its course without the possibility of diverting it. Its progress is imperceptible to the man who is not formed to observe it; but it does not escape the attention of the Philosopher."

"I am thinking of establishing, in the next degree, a sort of an academy of Literati. My design would include the study of the Ancients, and an application to the art of observing and drawing characters (even those of the living); and treatises and questions, proposed for public compositions, should form the occupations of our pupils. — I should wish, more especially, to make them spies over each other in particular, and over all in general. It is from this class that I would select those who have shown the greatest aptness for the Mysteries. My determination, in short, is, that in this degree they shall labour at the discovery and extirpation of prejudices. Every pupil (for example) shall declare, at least once a month, all those which he may have discovered in himself; which may have been his principal one, and how far he has been able to get the better of it."

"There certainly exist in the world public crimes which every wife and honest man would wish to suppress. When we consider that every man in this delightful world might be happy, but that their happiness is prevented by the misfortunes of some, and by the crimes and errors of others; that the wicked have power over the good; that opposition or partial insurrection is useless; that hardships generally fall upon men of worth;—then naturally results the wish of seeing an association formed of men of vigorous and noble minds, capable of resisting the wicked, of succouring the good, and of procuring for themselves rest, content and safety—of producing all these effects, by means drawn from the greatest degree of force of which human nature is capable. Such views actuating a Secret Society would not only be innocent, but most worthy of the wise and well-inclined man."

"This empire once established by means of the union and multitude of the adepts, let force succeed to the invisible power. Tie the hands of those who resist; subdue and stifle wickedness in the germ;"

"What these men [The Jesuits] have done for the Altar and the Throne why would not I do in opposition to the Altar and the Throne? With legions of adepts subject to my laws, and by the lure of mysteries, why may not I destroy under the cover of darkness, what they edified in broad day? What Christ even did for God and for Cæsar, why shall not I do against God and Cæsar, by means of adepts now become my apostles?"

"What will numbers avail us, if unity and similarity of sentiment do not prevail? — No rank, no state of life, can dispense the Brethren from our labours or our trials. To accustom them to despise all distinctions, and to view the world and human nature in the grand scale, the Prefect shall carefully collect all the anecdotes he can, remarkable either for their generosity or meanness, not regarding to whom they relate, whether Princes or Citizens, rich or poor. He will transmit them to the Masters of the Minervals; and these will expose them in a proper manner to their pupils. They will not forget to give the name of the Prince of great personage, though the trait should dishonour him; for every member must be made sensible, that we distribute impartial justice, and that among us the wicked man upon the throne is called a villain (ein schurke heist) just as freely, if not more so, than the criminal who is being led to the gallows."

"Hence the pupils will constantly accord themselves in every thing, whether in language or action, with the Superiors, though their motives may be unknown to them. But these means we shall all tend toward the same object; the young adepts will accustom themselves to search and dive into the intentions of the Order; to refrain from acting; or to be silent on all doubtful occasions, till they have received the advice or orders of their Superior as to what they ought to do or say."

"try to keep our pupils constantly occupied with objects relating to the Order; make it their favourite pursuit. — See what the Roman Catholic Church does to make its religion familiar to its followers, how it keeps their attention incessantly toward it; model yourself by that.—It would be impossible to foresee all cases and lay down rules for them;—Let it then be the constant study of the Prefects and other Superiors to prepare themselves for unforeseen events—Let them propose and distribute prizes for the best compositions on such cases. Perpetual vigilance will render it impossible for the edifice not sooner or later to succeed, and to take a proper consistency according to the local circumstances. Exhort the Brethren to complacency, beneficence, and generosity toward each other and toward the Order."

"That should he have been diligent and successful in impressing the young pupils with the grandeur of the views of the Sect, they will doubtless obey the Superiors with pleasure. How can they do otherwise than submit themselves to be conducted by Superiors who have so carefully guided them hitherto, who contributed so much to their present happiness, and who promise to perpetuate it in future? May the man who is not to be enticed into obedience by such advantages be rejected from among us; let him be cast out from the society of the elect! The spirit of obedience is to be more particularly infused by example and instruction—by the conviction, that to obey our Superiors is in fact only fulfilling our own inclination—by the gradual progress of the degrees—by the hopes of discovering more important truths—by fear properly managed—by honours, rewards, and distinctions granted to the docile—by contempt cast on the stubborn—by avoiding familiarity with the inferiors—by the exemplary punishment of the rebellious—by the selection of those whom we know to be devoted to us and ready to execute all our commands—by a particular attention to the Quibus Licets whereby we may see how far the Orders of the Superiors have been executed;—and by the punctuality of the intermediary Superiors in sending the tablets or reports respecting their inferiors. The more particular those tablets are, the better they will be; for it is on them that all the operations of the Order are grounded. It is by their means that the progress and number of the Brethren are to be known; that the strength or weakness of the machine, and the proportion and adhesion of all its parts are to be calculated, and that the promotion of the Brethren, the merits and demerits of the assemblies, of the Lodges, and of their Superiors, are to be judged.

"The Prefect is informed, that this is the most essential article; and it is on that account that even in countries where the Sect may have acquired sufficient power to throw off its mask, it is to remain veiled in darkness."

"The Prefect is always to hide with dexterity the real object of his views according to local circumstances. Let him agree with the Provincial on what shape he shall assume to conceal the Order. As in the religious institutions of the Roman Church, where religion, alas! is but a pretext; exactly so, only in a nobler manner, must we enwrap our Order in the forms of a mercantile society, or some other exterior of a similar nature."

"Lest the number of the Brethren should expose them to discovery, by their assemblies being too numerous, the Prefect will take care that no more than ten members shall assemble in the same Minerval Church."

"Should any place contain a greater number of pupils, the Lodges must be multiplied, or different days of assembly must be assigned, that all may not meet at once; and should there be several Minerval Churches in the same town, the Prefect will take care that those of one Lodge shall know nothing of the others."

"It has already been stated in the rules, that persons not belonging to the Order may be received into the Masonic Lodges of Illuminism — The Prefect will carefully watch lest any of these strangers should take the lead in the Lodges. — They should as far as possible be honest men, sedate, and quiet; but by some means or other they should be made useful to the Order. — Without leave of the Provincial, the Prefect shall hold no correspondence on matters relating to the Order with any person out of his province — as his peculiar object will be, to watch over and to instruct the Superiors of the Minerval and Masonic Lodges, he will have recourse to the Provincial in all doubtful cases of any importance.

"Let the Prefect make himself perfect master of these rules; let him follow them with precision; let him always attend to the whole of the object; let him take care that each one may attend to his duty, doing neither more nor less than the law requires; and he will find in this instruction all that is necessary for the regulation of his conduct."

"If, it is said, we have exactly foreseen every thing relating to these five articles, nothing will be impossible for us in any country under the Sun."

"The Scotch Knights are to pay particular attention to the discovery of any plans which may contribute to fill the coffers of the Order. It were much to be wished that they could devise means of putting the Order into possession of some considerable revenues in their province. — He that shall have rendered so signal a service must never hesitate at believing that these revenues are employed in the most noble purposes.— The whole must labour with all their might to consolidate the edifice little by little within their district, until the finances of the Order shall be found to be competent to its views."

"The Scotch Knights shall be particularly attentive that the Major Illuminees do not neglect to mention in their monthly letters such employments as they may have to dispose of."

"In every town of any note situated within their district, the Secret Chapters shall establish Lodges for the three ordinary degrees, and shall cause men of sound morals, of good repute, and of easy circumstances, to be received in these Lodges. Such men are much to be sought after, and are to be made Masons, even though they should not be of any service to Illuminism in its ulterior projects."

"If there already exists a Lodge in any given town, the Knights of Illuminism must find means of establishing a more legitimate one; at least, they should spare no pains to gain the ascendancy in those which they find established, either to reform or to destroy them."

"They must strongly exhort the members of our lodges not to frequent (without leave of their Superiors) any of those pretended constituted lodges, who hold nothing of the English but their diplomas, and some few symbols and ceremonies which they do not understand. All such Brethren are perfectly ignorant of true Masonry, of its grand object, and its real patrons. Though some of the greatest merit are to be found in such lodges, we nevertheless have strong reasons for not readily allowing them to visit ours."

"Our Scotch Knights must pay great attention to the regularity of the subordinate lodges, and must above all things attend to the preparation of candidates. It is here that in a private intercourse they will show a man that they have probed him to the quick. Surprise him by some ensnaring question in order to observe whether he has any presence of mind. If he be not staunch to his principles, and should expose his weak side, make him feel how great his necessities are, and how necessary it is for him to be guided entirely by us."

"The Deputy Master of the Lodge (who is generally the auditor of the accounts) must also be a member of our Secret Chapter. He will persuade the lodges that they alone dispose of their funds; but he will take care to employ them according to the views of the Order. Should it at any time be necesssary to help one of our brethren, the proposition is made to the lodge; though the brother should not even be a Mason, no matter, some expedient must be found to carry the point."

"No part of the capital, however, must in any case be alienated, that hereafter we may find the necessary funds for the most important undertakings. The tenth part of the subscriptions of these lodges must be annually carried to the Secret Chapter. The treasurer to whom these funds must be transmitted, shall collect them, and endeavour by all kinds of expedients to augment them."

"But before any part of our own funds are appropriated to the help of any of our Brethren, every effort shall be made to procure the necessary succours from the funds belonging to lodges which do not pertain to our system. — In general, the money which these lodges spend in a useless manner, should be converted to the advancement of our grand object."

"Whenever a learned Mason shall enter our Order, he must be put under the immediate direction of our Scotch Knights."

"[Baron Von Knigge:] To unite these two classes of men, to make them concur and co-operate toward our object, it was necessary to represent Christianity in such a light as to recall the superstitious to reason, and to teach our more enlightened sages not to reject it on account of its abuse. This should have been the secret of Masonry, and have led us to our object. Meanwhile despotism strengthens daily, though liberty universally keeps pace with it. It was necessary then to unite the extremes. We therefore assert here, that Christ did not establish a new religion, but that his intention was simply to reinstate natural religion in its rights; that by giving a general bond of union to the world, by diffusing the light and wisdom of his morality, and by dissipating prejudices, his intention was, to teach us the means of governing ourselves, and to re-establish, without the violent means of revolutions, the reign of Equality and Liberty among men. This was easily done by quoting certain texts from Scripture, and by giving explanations of them, true or false is of little consequence, provided each one finds a sense in these doctrines of Christ consonant with his reason. We add, that this religion, so simple in itself, was afterwards defaced; but that, by means of inviolable secrecy, it has been transmitted in purity to us through Freemasonry. Spartacus (Weishaupt) had collected many materials for this, and I added my discoveries in the instructions for these two degrees. Our people, therefore, being convinced that we alone are possessed of the real secrets of Christianity, we have but to add a few words against the Clergy and Princes. In the last mysteries we have to unfold to our adepts this pious fraud, and then by writings demonstrate the origin of all religious impositions, and their mutual connexion with each other."

"One might be tempted to think that this degree [that of Epopt or Priest] was the last and the most sublime: I have, nevertheless, three more of infinitely greater importance, which I reserve for our Grand Mysteries. But these I keep at home, and only show them to the Areopagites, or to a few other brethren the most distinguished for their merit and their services. — Were you here, I would admit you to my degree, for you are worthy of it — But I never suffer it to go out of my hands. It is of too serious an import; it is the key of the ancient and modern, the religious and political history of the universe."

"That I may keep our provinces in due subordination, I will take care to have only three copies of this degree in all Germany; that is to say, one in each Inspection."

"I have composed four more degrees above that of Regent; and with respect to these four, even the lowest of them, our degree of Priest will be but child's play"

"The illuminized Priests, or Epopts, are presided over by a Dean chosen by themselves. They are to be known to the inferior degrees only under the appellation of Epopt — their meetings are called Synods. All the Epopts within the circle of the same district compose a Synod; but each district shall contain no more than nine Epopts, exclusive of the Dean and Prefect of the Chapter. The higher superiors may attend these Synods."

"Of the nine Epopts, seven preside over the sciences distributed under as many heads in the following order:

"I. Physics. — Under this head are comprehended Dioptrics, Catoptrics, Hydraulics and Hydrostatics; Electricity, Magnetism, Attraction, &c."

"II. Medicine — comprising Anatomy, Chirurgery, Chym-istry, &c."

"III. Mathematics. — Algebra; Architecture, civil and mili-tary; Navigation, Mechanics, Astronomy, &c."

"IV. Natural History. — Agriculture, Gardening, Economics, the Knowledge of Insects and Animals including Man, Mineralogy, Metallurgy, Geology, and the science of the earthly phenomena."

"V. Politics — which embraces the study of Man, a branch in which the Major Illuminées furnish the materials; Geography, History, Biography, Antiquity, Diplomatics; the political history of Orders, their design, their progress, and their mutual dissentions." This last article seems to have the divers Orders of Masonry in view. A nota bene is added in the original, with a particular injunction to attend to this article, which the dissentions of the Illuminees and Freemasons had probably rendered of great importance to the Sect.

"VI. The Arts.—Mechanics, Painting, Sculpture, Engraving, Music, Dancing, Eloquence, Poetry, Rhetoric, all the branches of Literature; the Trades."

"VII. The Occult Sciences.—The study of the Oriental tongues, and others little known, the secret methods of writing, the art of decyphering; the art of raising the seals of the letters of others, and that of preserving their own from similar practices; The study of ancient and modern hieroglyphics; and, once more, of secret societies, Masonic systems, &c. &c."

"As often as your own knowledge and that of your pupils shall not suffice, you may ask the advice of learned strangers, and turn their knowledge to the advantage of our Order, but without letting them perceive it. This precaution is the more to be insisted on, as one of the grand objects of the Epopts must be, "to attain such perfection in science, that Illuminism shall never be beholden to the prophane; but that the latter, on the contrary, shall perpetually stand in need of the lights of the Order."

"The Epopt must keep a list of a very great number of important questions proper for investigation, and which he may eventually propose to the young adepts.—In the branch of practical Philosophy, for example, he will propose for investigation the question, how far the principle is true, that all means are allowable, when employed for a laudable end? How far this maxim is to be limited to keep the proper medium between Jesuitical abuse, and the scrupulosity of prejudice? Questions of this nature shall be sent to the Dean, who shall transmit them to the Minerval schools for the investigation of the young adepts, and their dissertations will swarm with a multitude of ideas, new, bold, and useful, which will greatly enrich our Magazine."

"For example at the Letter C in the register of secret sciences and hieroglyphics the word Cross is to be found, and under it is the following note—For the antiquity of this hieroglyphic, consult such a work, printed such a year, such a page, or else such a manuscript, signature M."

"By means of these and such like observations, the Order will be enabled to make discoveries of every kind, to form new systems, and to give on all subjects irrefragable proofs of its labours and its immense fund of science; and the public will give it credit for being in possession of all human knowledge."

"Particular parts of these sciences and discoveries may be printed by permission of the Superiors; but the law adds, not only these books shall not be communicated to any of the prophane, but as they will never be printed elsewhere than at the presses of the Sect, they will only be entrusted to the Brethren according to the rank they hold in the Order."

"That our worthy co-operators may not be divested of the glory of their labours, every new principle laid down, machine invented, or discovery made, shall for ever bear the name of its inventor, that his memory may be revered by future ages."

"On the same grounds it is strictly enjoined, that no member shall ever communicate to the prophane any discovery that he may have made in the Order—No book treating of these discoveries shall be printed without the permission of the Superiors; and hence arises the general regulation, that no Brother shall publish any of his productions without leave of the Provincial. He also is to decide whether the work is of a nature to be printed by the secret presses of the Order, and what particular Brethren may be allowed the perusal of it—Should it be necessary to dismiss any of the Brethren from the Order, the local Superior is to receive notice that he may have the necessary time to withdraw from him not only the manuscripts, but even the printed works of the Order."

"The wants of every country are to be maturely considered, as well as those of your district; let them be the objects of deliberation in your Synods; and ask instructions of your Superiors."

"You will incessantly form new plans, and try every means, in your respective provinces, to seize upon the public education, the ecclesiastical government, the chairs of literature, and the pulpit."

"the Epopt must find means of acquiring the reputation of a man of transcendent learning; wherever he appears, whether walking or stopping, sitting or standing, let rays of light encircle his head, which shall enlighten all who approach him. Let every one think himself happy in hearing the pure truth from his lips. Let him on all occasions, combat prejudice; but with precaution, and according to the rules laid down, with dexterity and with all the respect due to the persons he is addressing."

"In the literary world certain writings generally take the lead for a time, according to the fashion, and inspire feeble minds with admiration. At one time the enthusiastic productions of Religion, at another the sentimental novels of wit, or perhaps philosophical reveries, pastorals, romances on chivalry, epic poems, or odes, will inundate the republic of letters. The Epopt will turn all his skill toward bringing into fashion the principles of our Order, the sole tendency of which is the happiness of mankind."

"Our principles must be made fashionable, that the young writers may diffuse them among the people, and serve the Order without intending it."

"In order to raise the public spirit, he must with the greatest ardour preach up the general interest of humanity, and inculcate the utmost indifference for all associations or secret unions which are only formed among the subjects of one particular nation."

"He will take care that the writings of the members of the Order shall be cried up, and that the trumpet of fame shall be sounded in their honour. He will also find means of hindering the reviewers from casting any suspicions on the writers of the Sect."

"You must infuse so great a respect for the sublimity and sanctity of our Order, that a promise made by the adepts on the honour of Illuminism shall be more binding than the most sacred oath."

"He who shall dare violate the oath he shall have sworn on the honour of my Society, shall be declared infamous. I care not what his rank may be, his infamy shall be proclaimed throughout the whole Order, and it shall be so without remission or hope of pardon. My intention is, that the Members should be informed of this, that they should deliberately reflect on the sacredness of this oath in my Order, I mean that the consequences of it should be clearly and warmly represented to them."

"When one of our Epopts has sufficiently distinguished himself to bear a part in the political government of our Order; that is to say, when he unites prudence with the liberty of thinking and of acting; when he knows how to temper boldness with precaution, resolution with complaisance; subtlety with good nature; loyalty with simplicity; singularity with method; transcendency of wit with gravity and dignity of manners; when he has learned opportunely to speak or to be silent, how to obey or to command; when he shall have gained the esteem and affection of his fellow-citizens, though feared by them at the same time; when his heart shall be entirely devoted to the interests of our Order, and the common welfare of the universe shall be uppermost in his mind; then, and only then, let the Superior of the province propose him to the National Inspector as worthy of being admitted to the degree of Regent."

"Three things of the utmost consequence are to be observed. In the first place, the greatest reserve is necesssary with respect to this degree. Secondly, those who are admitted into it must be as much as possible free men and independent of all Princes: they must indeed have clearly manifested their hatred for the general constitution or the actual state of mankind; have shown how ardently they wish for a change in the government of the world; and how much the hints thrown out in the degree of Priest has inflamed their wishes for a better order of things."

"I firmly believe, that the secret doctrine of Christ had no other object in view than the re-establishment of Jewish Liberty, which is the explanation I give of it. I even believe, that Freemasonry is nothing but a Christianity of this sort; at least, my explanation of their Hieroglyphics perfectly coincides with such an explanation. In this sense, nobody could blush at being a Christian; for I preserve the name, and substitute reason.  It is no trivial matter to have discovered a new Religion and a new Polity in these tenebrous Hieroglyphics. One might be induced to think that this was my highest degree; I have, nevertheless, three of infinitely more importance, for our grand mysteries."

"You know that the Unity of God was one of the secrets revealed in the mysteries of Eleusis; as for that, there is no fear of any such thing being found in mine."

"With our beginners let us act prudently with respect to books on Religion and Polity. In my plan, I reserve them for the grand mysteries. At first we must put only books of history or of metaphysics into their hands. Let Morality be our pursuit. Robinet, Mirabeau (that is to say, the System of Nature written by Diderot, though attributed to Mirabeau), the Social System, Natural Polity, the Philosophy of Nature, and such works, are reserved for my higher degrees. — At present they must not even be mentioned to our adepts, and particularly Helvetius on Man."

"Do put Brother Numenius in correspondence with me; I must try to cure him of his Theosophical ideas, and properly prepare him for our views."

"He who wishes to labour for the happiness of mankind, to add to the content and rest of the human species, to decrease their dissatisfaction must scrutinize and weaken those principles which trouble their rest, contentment, and happiness. Of this species are all those systems which are hostile to the ennobling and perfecting of human nature; which unnecessarily multiply evil in the world, or represent it as greater than it really is: all those systems which depreciate the merit and the dignity of man, which diminish his confidence in his own natural powers, and thereby render him lazy, pusillanimous, mean, and cringing: all those also which beget enthusiasm, which bring human reason into discredit, and thus open a free course for imposture: All the Theosophical and Mystical Systems; all those which have a direct or indirect tendency to such Systems; in short, all the principles derived from Theosophy, which, concealed in our hearts, often finish by leading men back to it, belong to this class."

"After having thus shown to our people that we are the real Christians, we have only a word to add against Priests and Princes. I have made use of such precaution in the degrees of Epopt and of Regent, that I should not be afraid of conferring them on Kings or Popes, provided they had undergone the proper previous trials. In our last mysteries we have to acknowledge this pious fraud; to prove, upon the testimony of authors, the origin of all the religious impostures, and to expose the whole with their connections and dependencies."

"With respect to the two degrees of Mage and of Man King, there is no reception, that is to say, there are no ceremonies of initiation. Even the Elect are not permitted to transcribe these degrees, they only hear them read;

and that is the reason why I do not publish them with this work."

"The first is that of Mage, also called Philosopher. It contains the fundamental principles of Spinozism. Here every thing is material; God and the world are but one and the same thing; all religions are inconsistent, chimerical, and the invention of ambitious men."

"The second degree of the grand mysteries, called the Man King, teaches that every inhabitant of the country or town, every father of a family, is sovereign, as men formerly were in the times of the patriarchal life, to which mankind is once more to be carried back; that, in consequence, all authority and all magistracy must be destroyed. — I have read these two degrees, and have passed through all those of the Order."

"If among our Epopts any speculative geniuses are to be found, they shall be admitted to the degree of Mage. — These adepts shall be employed in collecting and digesting all the grand philosophical systems, and will invent or compile for the people a system of religion which our Order means as soon as possible to give to the universe."

"In every nation there shall be a National Director associated and in direct communication with our Fathers, the first of whom holds the helm of the Order."

"Their labours, with regard to the parts purely speculative, were to have in view the knowledge and the tradition of all the important, holy, and sublime discoveries to be made in the religious mysteries and in the higher philosophy. Twelve Areopagites only are to compose this tribunal; and one of them is to be the chief. When any one of the members dies, or retires, his successor is chosen from among the Regents."

"It is by these means that I discover such of our Order as have the proper dispositions for adopting certain special doctrines, and more elevated, on governments and religious opinions."

"The maxims and politics of the Order are completely explained in the end. Here, in the Supreme Council, they project and examine the plans to be adopted for gradually enabling us to attack the enemy of reason and human nature personally. Here also the mode of introducing such plans into the Order is discussed, and it is decided to which brethren they are to be entrusted, and how far each one can be employed in their execution, in proportion to the insight given to him."

"The Areopagites shall form the Supreme Council. Their occupations shall relate to affairs of the greatest importance, and they shall pay little or no attention to such as are less essential. — They may recruit, it is true; that is to say, they may entice Candidates into the Order; but they must leave the care of their instruction to some intelligent adept. From time to time they will visit these Candidates, to inspire them with fresh ardour, to stimulate their zeal — They will be particularly careful in seeing that the progress and method of our Illuminées is every where uniform — They will more particularly watch over Athens (Munich). They will make no reports concerning that Lodge to any body but Spartacus. They will send monthly a statement of all the principal events, a sort of Gazette to the Brethren; that is to say, to those only who are initiated in the last secrets. But nota bene, this Gazette as yet has been no more than our common journal; the Brethren must compose one for the use of the Areopagites. These latter will labour at projects, ameliorations, and other objects of a similar nature, which are to be made known to the Brethren by circular letters. They are the people who are to bear a part of the weight of the general correspondence—They are not allowed to open the letters of complaint; that is to say, those containing any complaints against them. These are to be transmitted to the general, to Spartacus, as a sure means of informing him that they fulfil their duty. This instruction being only provisional, and relating solely to the Areopage, shall not be circulated; but the council will take a copy and send back the Original to Spartacus.

"The assembling of the council is to be regulated according to the feasts marked in the calendar of the Order."

"Silence and secrecy are the very soul of the Order, and you will carefully observe this silence as well with those whom you may have only reason to suppose are already initiated, as with those whom you may hereafter know really to belong to the Order. You will remember, that it is a constant principle among us, that ingenuousness is only a virtue with respect to our superiors, but that distrust and reserve are the fundamental principles. You will never reveal to any person, at present or hereafter, the slightest circumstance relative to your admission into the order, the degree you have received, nor the time when admitted; in a word, you will never speak of any object relating to the order even before Brethren, without the strongest necessity."

"This machine of ours must be so perfectly simple that a child could direct it."

## On the Selection of Candidates for Initiation

"Our strength chiefly consists in numbers; but much will also depend on the means employed to form the pupil — Young people are pliant and easily take the impression. The Prefect will therefore spare no pains to gain possession of the Schools which lie within his district, and also of their teachers. He will find means of placing them under the tuition of members of our Order; for this is the true method of infusing our principles and of training our young men: it is thus that the most ingenious men are prepared to labour for us and are brought into discipline; and thus that the affection conceived by our young pupils for the Order will gain as deep root as do all other early impressions."

"When a new colony is to be founded, begin by choosing a bold and enterprizing adept entirely devoted to the Order. Send him some time beforehand to live on the spot where you intend making the new establishment."

"Before you proceed to people the extremities, begin by making your ground good at the centre."

"Your next object must be, to gain over such persons as are constant residents, as Merchants and Canons."

"Such missions should only be entrusted to brethren of independent fortune, and who would occasion no expence to the Order; for though all the brethren are entitled to succour when in real want, yet those of one province are as seldom as possible to be an expence to the neighbouring ones. Nor are the other districts by any means to be made acquainted with the weakness of the

Order in yours. Beside, the funds must find a sufficiency to succour those of the Minerval school who may stand in need of it, that our promises in their case may be performed."

"You will not seek to extend yourself till you have consolidated your establishment in the capital of your district."

You will seriously examine and cautiously select from the Brethren those who are the most able to undertake such a mission. You will next consider whether it will be proper to begin your establishment by a Minerval Church or a Masonic Lodge."

"Pay most particular attention to the man whom you place at the head of the new colony; observe whether he is courageous, zealous, prudent, exact, and punctual; whether fitted for the forming new adepts; whether he enjoys a good reputation or is much considered; whether he is a man of business and capable of a serious and constant application; in short, whether he has all the necessary qualifications for an undertaking of such high importance."

"Consider also the locality. Is the place proposed near to or distant from the capital of your district? — Is it a dangerous or safe situation for such an undertaking? — Is it great or small, more or less populous? — By what means can you best succeed, and which can be easiest employed? — What time would be requisite for the perfecting of such an establishment? — To what persons can you apply on first setting off? — If your first applications be ill made, all future attempts will be fruitless. — What pretence or what name is to be assumed?—How is the new colony to be subordinated or co-ordinated? that is to say, what Superiors shall it be under, and with what Lodges shall it correspond?"

"When you shall have acquired sufficient strength in your new colony, and particularly if our Brethren enjoy the first dignities of the state, if they may freely and openly show themselves formidable to their opponents, and make them feel the painful consequences of counteracting the views of the Order; if you have wherewith to satisfy the wants of the Brethren; if, so far from having to fear from the government, the Order directs those who hold the reins—Then be assured that we shall not be wanting in numbers or in the choice of adepts; we shall soon have more than we have occasion for. I cannot too strongly recommend this method of proceeding."

"If it be necessary for us to be masters of the ordinary schools, of how much more importance will it be to gain over the ecclesiastical seminaries and their superiors! With them, we gain over the chief part of the country; we acquire the support of the greatest enemies to innovation; and the grand point of all is, that through the clergy we become masters of the middle and lower classes of the people."

"But remember that great caution is necessary with the Ecclesiastics. These gentlemen are generally either too free or too scrupulous; and those who are too free have seldom any morals."

"When the Prefect shall have gradually succeeded in placing the most zealous members of the Order in the councils and offices under the Prince, he will have arrived at the full extent of his commission. He will have done much more than if he had initiated the Prince himself."

"In general, Princes are not to be admitted into the Order, and even those who are received are seldom to be permitted to rise above the degree of Scotch Knight."

"Leave those brutes, those clownish and thickheaded fellows!"

"Seek me out, for example, the dexterous and dashing youths. We must have adepts who are insinuating, intriguing, full of resource, bold and enterprising; they must also be flexible and tractable, obedient, docile, and sociable. Seek out also those who are distinguished by their power, nobility, riches, or learning, nobiles, potentes, divites, doctos, quærite—Spare no pains, spare nothing in the acquisition of such adepts. If heaven refuse its aidance, conjure hell.

"[Of rich but stupid people] These are a good sort of beings, they are necessary beings. They augment our number and fill our coffers, augent numerum et ærarium. Courage then! and make these gentry swallow the bait; but beware of communicating to them our secrets; For this species of adept must always be persuaded that the degree they are in is the highest."

"[Of professionals: lawyers, doctors etc.] Those are worth having, but they are sometimes real devils, so difficult are they to be led; they however are worth having when they can be gained over."

"He will spare no trouble to gain the Prince's officers, whether presiding over provinces, or attending him in his councils. He that has succeeded in this has done more, than if he had engaged the Prince himself. In fine, the Provincial, or the chief Insinuator, is to recruit every thing that can be tainted with Illuminism, or can be serviceable to its cause."

"Above all things pay attention to the figure, and select the well-made men and handsome young fellows. They are generally of engaging manners and nice feelings. When properly formed, they are the best adapted for negotiations; for first appearances prepossess in their favour. It is true, they have not the depth that men of more gloomy countenances often have. They are not the persons to be entrusted with a revolt, or the care of stirring up the people; but it is for that very reason that we must know how to choose our agents. I am particularly fond of those men whose very soul is painted in their eyes, whose foreheads are high, and whose countenances are open. Above all, examine well the eyes, for they are the very mirrors of the heart and soul. Observe the look, the gait, the voice. Every external appearance leads us to distinguish those who are fit for our school."

"Select those in particular who have met with mis-fortunes, not from accidents, but by some act of injustice; that is to say, in other words, the discontented; for such are the men to be called into the bosom of Illuminism, as into their proper asylum."

"Be careful lest your own inclinations should bias your judgment. Do not think a man excellent because he has a brilliant quality, nor judge him to be wicked because he has some striking defect: for that is the grand failing of those who are captivated at first sight."

"Above all, guard against believing your man to be a transcendent genius because his discourse is brilliant. We are to judge by facts alone, whether a man is deeply interested."

"Have little confidence in rich or powerful men; their conversion is very slow."

"On the Physiognomy of the Candidate:—Is he of a florid complexion, or pale? Is he white, black, fair, or brown? Is his eye quick, piercing, dull, languishing, amorous, haughty, ardent, or dejected? In speaking, does he look full in the face and boldly, or does he look sideways? Can he endure being stared full in the face? Is his look crafty, or is it open and free; is it gloomy and pensive, or is it absent, light, insignificant, friendly, or serious? Is his eye hollow, or level with the head, or does it stare? His forehead, is it wrinkled, and how; perpendicularly, or horizontally? &c.

"His Countenance:—Is it noble or common, open, easy, or constrained? How does he carry his head; erect or inclined, before, behind, or on one side, firm or shaking, sunk between his shoulders, or turning from one side to the other? &c.

"His Gait:—Is it slow, quick, or firm? Are his steps long, short, dragging, lazy, or skipping? &c.

"His Language:—Is it regular, disorderly, or interrupted? In speaking, does he agitate his hands, his head, or his body, with vivacity? Does he close upon the person he is speaking to? Does he hold them by the arm, clothes, or button-hole? Is he a great talker, or is he taciturn? If so, why? Is it through prudence, ignorance, respect, or sloth? &c.

"His Education:—To whom does he owe it? Has he always been under the eyes of his parents? How has he been brought up, and by whom? Has he any esteem for his masters? To whom does he think himself indebted for his education? Has he travelled, and in what countries?"

"When he finds himself with different parties, which does he adopt, the strongest or the weakest, the wittiest or the most stupid? Or does he form a third? Is he constant and firm in spite of all obstacles? How is he to be gained, by praise, flattery, or low courtship; or by women, money, or the entreaties of his friends?" &c.—

"Whether he loves satire, and on what he exercises that talent; on religion, superstition, hypocrisy, intolerance, government, ministers, monks?" &c.

What is the character of a man whose eyes are perpetually in motion, and whose countenance is changeable? What features denote voluptuousness, melancholy, and pusillanimity?"

## On the Instruction of Candidates for Initiation

"The grand art of rendering any revolution whatsoever certain—is to enlighten the people;—and to enlighten them is, insensibly to turn the public opinion to the adoption of those changes which are the given object of the intended revolution."

"According to my views, I cannot employ men as they are; I must form them; each class of my Order must be a preparatory school for the next; and all this must necessarily be the work of time."

"When that object cannot be promulgated without exposing him that has conceived it to public vengeance, he must know how to propagate his opinion in secret societies."

"When the object is an universal Revolution, all the members of these societies, aiming at the same point, and aiding each other, must find means of governing invisibly, and without any appearance of violent measures, not only the higher and more distinguished class of any particular state, but men of all stations, of all nations, and of every religion — Insinuate the same spirit every where — In silence, but with the greatest activity possible, direct the scattered inhabitants of the earth toward the same point."

"Apply yourselves to the acquiring of interior and exterior perfection;"

"Attend particularly to the art of dissembling and of disguising your actions, the better to observe those of others, and to penetrate into their inmost thoughts. "

"[the Illuminati insinuator must begin] by descanting on the supreme felicity of being versed in sciences which few can approach, of walking in the paths of light while the vulgar are groping in darkness. He must remark, that there exist doctrines solely transmitted by secret traditions, because they are above the comprehension of common minds. In proof of his assertions he will cite the

Gymnosophists in the Indies, the Priests of Isis in Egypt, and those of Eleusis and the Pythagorean school in Greece."

"Let him add, that all the sages of antiquity were acquainted with these doctrines; let him insist on the uncertainty that man is in with respect to the nature of the soul, its immortality, and its future destiny. He will then sound his candidate, to know whether he would not rejoice at having some satisfactory answers on objects of such great importance. At the same time he will hint that he has had the happiness of being initiated into these doctrines, and that, should the candidate wish it, he would do his best to procure him the same felicity; but that it was a science gradually imparted, and that certain men possessed the talent of guiding him from a distance, of leading him to the discovery of this new world, and that without being ever in his presence"

"Let your first care, be to gain the affection, the confidence, and the esteem of those persons whom you are to entice into the Order—let your whole conduct be such, that they shall surmise something more in you than you wish to show—hint that you belong to some secret and powerful society excite little by little, and not at once, a wish in your candidate to belong to a similar society— Certain arguments and certain books which the Insinuator must have, will greatly contribute to raise such a wish; such are, for example, those which treat of the union and strength of associations."

"One represents, for example, a child in the cradle; one speaks of its cries, its tears, its weakness—One remarks how this child, abandoned to itself, is entirely helpless; but that by the help of others it acquires strength—One shows how the greatness of Princes is derived from the union of their subjects—One exalts the advantages of the state of society over the state of nature—Then one touches on the art of knowing and directing mankind— How easily, you will say, could one man of parts lead hundreds, even thousands, if he but knew his own advantages. This is evidently proved by the organization of armies, and the amazing power which princes derive from the union of their subjects."

"When you shall have got thus far begin to show (as it were unguardedly) that you are not entirely ignorant of those secrets; throw out some half sentences which may denote it. Should your candidate take the hint, press him, and return to the charge, until you see him betray symptoms of a desire instantaneously to unite with such a society."

"The Insinuator, however, who has thus far succeeded in inspiring his pupil with such a wish, has not played off every engine with which the code has furnished him. To sound the very bottom of his mind, he will pretend to consult him as if he had been entrusted with certain secrets, he will make objections on the secrecy of these societies; but should they make too much impression he will resolve them himself. At other times, to stimulate the curiosity of his pupil, he will hold a letter in his hand written in cypher, or he will leave it half open on his table, giving his candidate sufficient time to observe the cypher, and then shut it up with all the air of a man who has important correspondences to keep secret. At other times studying the connections and actions of his pupil, he will tell him of certain circumstances which the young man will think he has learned by means of these secret societies, from whom nothing is hidden, though they are concealed from all the rest of the world."

"Learn also to act the valet in order to become master."

"[The superior should inquire] as to the books which he has read since the last meeting; on the observations or discoveries he may have made; and on his labours or services toward the progress of the Order."

"[The student should make a constant careful examination of his faults and mistakes] and it would be unpardonable neglect should any pupil pretend that during the space of a whole month he had remarked nothing reprehensible. This would be a proof of the utmost negligence in the training of his mind to observation; and the Superior must not suffer it to pass without reprehension. He must also make his observations in such a manner as to excite their serious attention, and effectually to impress them with proper notions, so that each on returning home shall be ready to put in practice his advice for the advantage of the Order."

"It is necessary that the adept look upon himself as the founder of the new Order"

"Assiduously observe every Brother entrusted to your care; watch him particularly on all occasions where he may be tempted not to be what he ought to be; that is precisely the moment when he must show himself; it is then that the progress he has made is to be discovered. Observe him again at those times when he least suspects it, when neither the desire of being praised, the fear of being blamed, nor the shame of, or reflexion on the punishment, can actuate his conduct. Be exact on such occasions in making your notes and observations. You will gain much both with respect to yourself and to your pupil."

"Your chief object must be to form the heart. He that is not deaf to the cries of the unfortunate; he that is constant though in adversity, and unshaken in his plans; he that feels his soul glow for great enterprizes; and he, particularly, who has formed his mind to observation, is the man of whom we are in quest. Reject those feeble and narrow minds who know not how to quit their usual sphere."

"Read with your pupils those books which are easy to be understood, which abound in the picturesque, and are calculated to elevate the mind. Speak to them often; but let your discourses proceed from the heart, and not from the head. Your auditors easily kindle when they see you full of fire. Make them thirst after the moment when the grand object is to be accomplished."

"Above all, stimulate them to the love of the object. Let them view it as grand, important, and congenial to their interests and favourite passions. Paint in strong colours the miseries of the world; tell them what men are, and what they might be; what line of conduct they should adopt; how little they know their own interests; how anxiously our society labours for them; and desire them to judge what they may expect from it, by what we have already done in the first degrees."

"Shun familiarity on all occasions where your weak side may be seen; always speak of Illuminism in a dignified style."

"Inspire esteem and respect for our Superiors; and dwell strongly on the necessity of obedience in a well-organized society."

"Kindle the ardour of your pupil by laying great stress on the utility of our labours; avoid dry and metaphysical discussions. Let what you require of your pupils be within their means. Study the peculiar habits of each; for men may be turned to any thing by him who knows how to take advantage of their ruling passions."

"To infuse into them a spirit of observation, begin by slight essays in conversation. Ask some easy questions on the means of discovering the character of a man notwithstanding all his dissimulation. Affect to think the answer a better one than you could have given yourself; that gives confidence, and you will find some other opportunity of delivering your own sentiments. Inform them of what observations you may have made concerning their voice, gait, or physiognomy. Tell them also, that they have the best dispositions, and that they only want practice. Praise some in order to stimulate others."

"Having thus become acquainted with the immense difficulty attending on the art of bringing men to the point whither you wished to lead them, neglect no occasion of disseminating the good principles wherever you can, and of inspiring your pupils with courage and resolution: but never forget, that he who wishes to convert too many at once will convert nobody. In the towns where you reside, divide the task with the other Illuminees of the same degree as yourself. Chuse one or two, at most three, Minervals among those over whom you have the greatest influence or authority; but spare neither labour nor pains. You will have accomplished a great undertaking if, during your whole life, you form but two or three men. Let those whom you have selected be the constant object of all your observations. When one method does not succeed, seek out another; and so on, till you have found a proper one. Study to find out what your pupil is best fitted for; in what intermediary principles he may be deficient, and therefore inaccessible to the fundamental ones. The grand art consists in profiting of the right moment; at one time it is warm, at another cool reasoning which will persuade. — Let your pupil always think that it is to himself, and not to you, that he is indebted for the progress he makes. If he falls in a passion, never contradict; hearken to him though he be in the wrong. Never controvert the consequences, but always the principle. Wait for a favourable moment when you may explain your sentiments without appearing to contradict his. The best method is to agree with another person, whom you will pretend to attack on those subjects, while the Candidate whom you really wish to convince is only a stander-by and takes no part in the dispute: then support your arguments with all the vigour of which you are capable.

"Whatever failings you wish to correct in him, speak of them as if they were not his; tell the story as if somebody else had been guilty of them; then take his advice on the subject; and by these means he becomes his own judge.

"All this, it is true, requires time: hurry nothing; it is solidity and facility of action that we want in our adepts. Often to read, meditate, hearken to, see the same thing, and then to act, is what gives that facility which soon becomes natural. . . ."

"Do you wish to draw forth his opinion? Propose a dissertation on certain questions relative to your object, as it were merely to exercise his genius. He thus learns how to meditate on the principles while you make a discovery of those which it is your object to eradicate from his mind."

"Instruct, advise; but beware of cold declamations: drop a few words to the purpose when you shall perceive his mind to be in a proper state to receive them."

"Never ask too much at once; let your conduct be provident, paternal, and solicitous. — Never despair; for one may do what one pleases with men.

"Make yourself master of the motives of the principles your pupil has acquired from his education. If they be not consonant with our views, weaken then by insensible gradations, and substitute and strengthen others. But great prudence is necessary to operate this."

"Observe what religions, sects, and politics, make men do. — One may enthusiastically wed them to follies; it is therefore in the manner of leading them that the whole art of giving the upper hand to virtue and truth consists. Only employ the same means for a good purpose which impostors employ for evil, and you will succeed. If the wicked are powerful, it is because the good are too timid and too indolent. There may be circumstances also, under which it will become necesssary to show dis-pleasure, and even anger, in defence of the rights of man."

"Tell your pupils, that they are only to attend to the purity of the views which actuate the Order; and that antiquity, power, or riches, should be perfectly indifferent to them."

"Tell them, that should they find elsewhere a society which would lead them with greater speed or with more certainty to the desired end, the Order would eternally regret the not having been acquainted with it before— That in the mean time we obey the laws of our Superiors, labouring in peace, and persecuting no man.— Follow these rules of conduct, and once more remember, that you will have rendered an essential service to the world, though you should form but two men according to our principles.

"Carefully profit of those moments when your pupil is discontented with the world, and when every thing goes contrary to his wishes; those moments when the most powerful man feels the want of the support of others, to attain a better order of things. It is then that you must press the swelling heart, stimulate the sensibility, and demonstrate how necessary secret societies are, for the attainment of a better order of things."

"But be not too easy in your belief with respect to the reality or constancy of such feelings. Indignation may be the effect of fear, or of the fleeting hopes of some passion which one wishes to gratify. Such feelings are not naturalized; men are not perfect in so short a time; prepare for the worst, and then insist. A heart which easily melts easily changes."

"Never promise too much, that you may be able to perform more than you promise. Rekindle exhausted courage; repress excessive ardour; inspire hope in misfortune, and fear in success."

"Such are the rules which will form you for a good preceptor and a leader of men. By an exact attention to them you will add to the number of the elect. If your own happiness be dear to you, labour (under our direction) at delivering many thousands of men, who wish to be good, from the dire necessity of being wicked.—Believe us, for it is the precept of experience, bereave vice of its power, and every thing will go well in this world: for if vice be powerful, it is only because one part of the good is too indolent, while the other is too ardent; or else, that men suffer themselves to be divided, or leave the care of Revolutions to futurity; the fact is, that in the mean time they had rather bend under the yoke, than efficaciously resist vice. If they once became sensible that virtue does not entirely consist in patience, but in action also, they would start from their sleep.— For your part, unite with the Brethren; place your confidence in our Society; nothing is impossible to it, if we follow its laws. We labour to secure to merit its just rewards; to the weak support, to the wicked the fetters they deserve; and to man his dignity. Such is the new Canaan, the new land of Promise, the land of abundance and blessing; though as yet, alas! we discover it but from a distance."

"That we may be uncontrolled in our discourse, let our pupils remark, that the Superiors enjoy a great latitude in that respect; that we sometimes speak in one way, sometimes in another; that we often question with great assurance only to sound the opinions of our pupils, and to give them an opportunity of showing it by their answers. This subterfuge repairs many errors. Let us always say, that the end will discover which of our observations conveys our true sentiments.—Thus we may speak sometimes in one way, at others in a quite different one, that we may never be embarrassed, and that our real sentiments may always be impenetrable to our inferiors. Let this be also inserted in the instructions, etiam hoc inseratur instructioni. It would still have a better effect, if you gave in charge to our Major Illuminees to vary their conversation with their inferiors, for the above reasons, ex rationibus supra dictis."

"I entreat that the maxims which are so often to be found in my letters may not be lost. Collect them for the use of our Areopagites, as they are not always present in my mind. With time they might form an excellent political degree. Philo has long since been employed about it. Communicate also your private instructions to each other, which may in time grow into an uniform Code. Read them attentively, that they may become familiar to you. Though I know them well and practise them they would take me too much time to digest them systematically. These maxims once engraved in your mind, you will enter better into my plans, and you will proceed more conformably to my mode of operation."

"Now I hold him; I defy him to hurt us; if he should wish to betray us, we have also his secrets."

# Extracts from Some of the Illuminati Initiation Rituals

## Novice Ritual

"[Written Oath] I, the undersigned, promise upon my honour, and without any reservation, never to reveal either by words, signs, or actions, or in any possible manner, to any person whatever, either relations, allies, or most intimate friends, any thing that shall be entrusted to me by my Introducer relative to my entrance into a secret society; and this whether my reception shall take place or not. I subject myself the more willingly to this secrecy, as my Introducer assures me that nothing is ever transacted in this society hurtful to religion, morals, or the state. With respect to all writings which I may be entrusted with, any letters which I may receive concerning the same object, I engage myself to return them, after having made for my sole use the necessary extracts."

"For the tranquillity and security of all the Brethren, whether Novices or active Members of the Society, and to prevent all ill-grounded suspicions, or disagreeable doubts, the venerable Order declares, that it absolutely has in view no project, enterprise, or undertaking hurtful to the state, to religion, or to good morals; and that it favours nothing of that nature in any of its members. Its designs, all its toils, solely tend to inspire men with a zeal for the perfection of their moral characters, to impregnate them with humane and sociable sentiments, to counteract the plans of the wicked, to succour oppressed and suffering virtue, to favour the advancement of men of merit, and to render those sciences universal which are as yet hidden from the generality of men. Such is not the coloured pretext, but the real object of the order."

"Our society exacts from its members the sacrifice of their liberty, not only with respect to all things, but absolutely with respect to every means of attaining its end. Yet the presumption on the goodness of the means prescribed is always in favour of the orders given by the superiors. They are clearer-sighted on this object; they are better acquainted with it; and it is on this very account that they are nominated superiors It is their business to lead you through the labyrinth of errors and darkness; and in such a case obedience is not only a duty, but an object for grateful acknowledgment."

I. Are you still desirous of being received into the Order of the Illuminees?

II. Have you seriously reflected on the importance of the step you take, in binding yourself by engagements that are unknown to you?

III. What hopes do you entertain, or, by what reasons are you induced to enter among us?

IV. Would you still persevere in that wish, though you should find that we had no other object or advantage whatever in view but the perfection of mankind?

V. What would be your conduct should the Order be of new invention?

VI. Should you ever discover in the Order any thing wicked, or unjust to be done, what part would you take?

VII. Can you and will you look upon the welfare of the Order as your own?

VIII. We cannot conceal from you, that Members, entering into our Order without any other motive than to acquire power, greatness, and consideration, are not those whom we prefer. In many cases one must know how to lose in order to gain. Are you aware of all this?

IX. Can you love all the Members of the Order, even such of your enemies as may be members of it?

X. Should it so happen that you should be obliged to do good to your enemies who are of the Order, to recommend them, for example, or extol them; would you be disposed to do so?

XI. Do you, moreover, grant the power of life and death to our Order or Society? On what grounds would you refuse, or recognize in it such a right?

XII. Are you disposed on all occasions to give the preference to men of our Order, over all other men?

XIII. How would you wish to revenge yourself of any injustice, either great or small, which you may have received from strangers or from any one of our Brethren?

XIV. What would be your conduct should you ever repent of having joined our Order?

XV. Are you willing to share with us happiness and misfortune?

XVI. Do you renounce the idea of ever making your birth, employment, station, or power, serve to the prejudice or contempt of any one of the Brethren?

XVII. Are you, or have you any idea of becoming a Member of any other society?

XVIII. Is it from levity, or in hopes of soon being acquainted with our constitution, that you so easily make these promises?

XIX. Are you fully determined to observe our laws?

XX. Do you subject yourself to a blind obedience without any restriction whatever? And do you know the strength of such an engagement?

XXI. Is there no consideration that can deter you from entering into our Order?

XXII. Will you, in case it is required, assist in the propagation of the Order, support it by your counsels, by your money, and by all other means?

XXIII. Had you any expectation that you would have to answer any of these questions; and if so, which question was it?

XXIV. What security can you give us that you will keep these promises; and to what punishment will you subject yourself in case you should break any of them?

"[Superior to Novice] Your request is just. In the name of the most Serene Order from which I hold my powers, and in the name of all its Members, I promise you protection, justice, and help. Moreover, I protest to you once more, that you will find nothing among us hurtful to Religion, to Morals, or to the State;"—here the Initiator takes in his hand the naked sword which lay upon the table, and, pointing it at the heart of the Novice, continues, "but should you ever be a traitor or a perjurer, assure yourself that every Brother will be called upon to arm against you. Do not flatter yourself with the possibility of escaping, or of finding a place of security. — Wherever thou mayst be, the rage of the Brethren, shame and remorse shall follow thee, and prey upon thy very entrails." — He lays down the sword. — "But if you persist in the design of being admitted into our Order, take this oath:"

"In presence of all powerful God, and of you Plenipotentiaries of the most high and most excellent Order into which I ask admittance, I acknowledge my natural weakness, and all the insufficiency of my strength. I confess that, notwithstanding all the privileges of rank, honours, titles, or riches which I may possess in civil society, I am but a man like other men; that I may lose them all by other mortals, as they have been acquired through them; that I am in absolute want of their approbation and of their esteem; and that I must do my utmost to deserve them both. I never will employ either the power or consequence that I may possess to the prejudice of the general welfare. I will, on the contrary, resist with all my might the enemies of human nature, and of civil society."

"I promise ardently to seize every opportunity of serving humanity, of improving my mind and my will, of employing all my useful accomplishments for the general good, in as much as the welfare and the statutes of the society shall require it of me.

"I vow an eternal silence, an inviolable obedience and fidelity to all my superiors and to the statutes of the Order. With respect to what may be the object of the Order I fully and absolutely renounce my own penetration and my own judgment.

"I promise to look upon the interests of the Order as my own; and as long as I shall be a Member of it, I promise to serve it with my life, my honour, and my estates. Should I ever, through imprudence, passion, or wickedness, act contrary to the laws or to the welfare of the Serene Order, I then subject myself to whatever punishment it may please to inflict upon me.

"I also promise to help the Order, to the best of my power, and according to my conscience, with my counsels and my actions, and without the least attention to my personal interest; also, to look upon all friends and enemies of the Order as my own, and to behave to them as the Order shall direct. I am equally disposed to labour with all my might and all my means at the propagation and advancement of the Order.

"In these promises I renounce every secret reservation, and engage to fulfill them all, according to the true purport of the words, and according to the signification attached to them by the Order when it prescribed the Oath—

"So help me God." N. N.

## Minor Illuminee Ritual

"You have given us a welcome and valuable proof of your confidence; but indeed we are not unworthy of it; and we hope that it will even increase in proportion as you become better acquainted with us. Among men whose sole object is to render themselves and others better, no dissimulation should subsist. Far be any reserve from us. We study the human heart—and do not hesitate or blush at revealing to each other our faults or errors. — Here then is the picture which the Lodge had drawn of your person. You must own that some features are not unlike. Read, and then answer, whether you still wish to belong to a society which (such as you are represented here) opens its arms to receive you."

"that he has still some few questions to answer, relative to objects on which it is absolutely necessary that the opinions of candidates should be known."

"I. Do you find that, in the world we live in, virtue is rewarded and vice punished? Do you not on the contrary observe, that the wicked man is exteriorly more comfortable, more considered, and more powerful, than the honest man? In a word, are you content with the world in its present situation?"

"II. In order to change the present order of things, would you not, if you had it in your power, assemble the good and closely unite them, in order to render them more powerful than the wicked?"

"III. If you had your choice, in what country would you wish to have been born rather than your own?"

"IV. In what age would you wish to have lived?"

"V. Always premising the liberty of choice, what science and what state of life would you prefer?"

"VI. With respect to history, who is your favourite author or your master?"

"VII. Do you not think yourself in duty bound to procure all the exterior advantages possible for your tried friends, in order to recompense them for their probity, and to render life more agreeable to them? Are you ready to do what the Order exacts of each member in this degree, when it ordains that each one shall bind himself to give advice every month to the Superiors, of the employments, support, benefices, or other such like dignities, of which he can dispose, or procure the possession by means of his recommendations; that the Superiors may present worthy subjects of our Order to all such employments?"

"Brother, you are a witness, that it is after having tried the best of men, that we seek little by little to reward them, and to give them support, that we may insensibly succeed in new modelling the world. Since you are convinced how imperfectly men have fulfilled their real destiny; how every thing has degenerated in their civil institutions; how little the teachers of wisdom and of truth have enhanced the value of virtue, or given a happier disposition to the world; you must be persuaded, that the error lies in the means which the sages have hitherto employed. Those means, therefore, must be changed, in order to reinstate in its rights the empire of truth and wisdom. And this is the grand object of the labours of our Order. Oh, my friend! my brother! my son! when here convened, far from the prophane, we consider to what an extent the world is abandoned to the yoke of the wicked, how persecution and misfortune is the lot of the honest man, and how the better part of human nature is sacrificed to personal interest. Can we at such a sight be silent, or content ourself with sighing? Shall we not attempt to shake off yoke?—Yes, my brother, rely upon us. Seek faithful co-operators, but seek them not in tumults and storms; they are hidden in darkness. Protected by the shades of night, solitary and silent, or reunited in small numbers, they, docile children, pursue the grand work under the direction of their Superiors. They call aloud to the children of the world, who pass by in the intoxication of pleasure — how few hearken to them! He alone who has the eye of the bird of Minerva, who has placed his labours under the protection of the star of night, is sure of finding them."

"To attain this we must trace the origin of all sciences; we must reward oppressed talents; we must raise from the dust the men of genius; we must undertake the education of youth; and, forming an indissoluble league among the most powerful geniuses, we must boldly, though with prudence, combat superstition, incredulity, and folly; and at length form our people to true, just, and uniform principles on all subjects.

"Such is the object of our Minerval Schools, and of the inferior degrees of Masonry, over which our Order wishes to acquire all the influence possible, in order to direct it towards our object. We also have our superior degrees, where the Brethren, after having passed through all the preparatory degrees, become acquainted with the ultimate result of the labours and of all the proceedings of the Order."

To obtain the completion of that result, "it will be necesssary to divest vice of its power, that the honest man may find his recompense even in this world; but in this grand project, we are counteracted by the Princes and the Priesthood; the political constitutions of nations oppose our proceedings. In such a state of things then what remains to be done? To instigate revolutions, overthrow every thing, oppose force to force, and exchange tyranny for tyranny? Far be from us such means. Every violent reform is to be blamed, because it will not ameliorate things as long as men remain as they are, a prey to their passions; and because wisdom needeth not the arm of violence."

"The whole plan of the Order tends to form men, not by declamation, but by the protection and rewards which are due to virtue. We must insensibly bind the hands of the protectors of disorder, and govern them without appearing to domineer."

"In a word, we must establish an universal empire over the whole world, without destroying the civil ties. Under this new empire, all other governments must be able to pursue their usual process, and to exercise every power, excepting that of hindering the Order from attaining its ends and rendering virtue triumphant over vice."

"This victory of virtue over vice was formerly the object of Christ, when he established his pure religion. He taught men, that the path to wisdom consisted in letting themselves be led for their greater good by the best and wisest men. At that time preaching might suffice; the novelty made truth prevail; but at present, more powerful means are necesssary. Man, a slave to his senses, must see sensible attractions in virtue. The source of passions is pure; it is necessary that every one should be able to gratify his within the bounds of virtue, and that our Order should furnish him with the means."

"It consequently follows, that all our brethren, educated on the same principles, and strictly united to each other, should have but one object in view. We must encompass the Power of the earth with a legion of indefatigable men, all directing their labours, according to the plan of the Order, towards the happiness of human nature—but all that is to be done in silence; our brethren are mutually to support each other, to succour the good labouring under oppression, and to seek to acquire those places which give power, for the good of the cause."

"Had we a certain number of such men in every country, each might form two others. Let them only be united, and nothing will be impossible to our Order; it is thus that in silence it has already performed much for the good of humanity."

"You behold, Brother, an immense field opening to your activity; become our faithful and worthy co-operator, by seconding us with all your might; and remember, that no service will pass without its just reward."

## Scotch Knight (or Directing Illuminee)

"[Initiator:] You here behold a part of those unknown legions which are united by indissoluble bonds to combat for the cause of humanity. Are you willing to make yourself worthy of watching with them for the sanctuary? Your heart must be pure, and a heavenly ardour for the dignity of nature must fire your breast. The step you are taking is the most important one of your life. Our games are not vainly ceremonial. In creating you a knight we expect of you that you will perform exploits grand, noble, and worthy of the title you receive. Long life to you, if you come to us to be faithful; if honest and good you answer our expectations. Should you prove a false Brother, be both cursed and unhappy, and may the grand Architect of the Universe hurl you into the bottomless pit! Now bend thy knee, and on this sword take the oath of the Order."

"[Oath] I promise obedience to the excellent Superiors of the Order. In as much as it shall depend upon me, I engage—never to favour the admission of any unworthy member into these holy degrees—to labour at rendering the Ancient Masonry triumphant over the false systems which have crept into it—to succour, like a true Knight, innocence, poverty, or oppressed honesty—Never to be the flatterer of the great, nor the slave of Princes;—to combat courageously, though prudently, in the cause of Virtue, Liberty, and Wisdom—to resist boldly, both for the advantage of the Order and of the world, Superstition and Despotism. I never will prefer my own private interest to that of the Order. I will defend my Brethren against calumny. I will dedicate my life to the discovery of the true Religion and real doctrines of Freemasonry, and I will impart my discoveries to my Superiors. I will disclose the secrets of my heart to my Superiors as to my best friends. So long as I shall remain in the Order I shall look upon the being a Member of it as a supreme felicity. I also engage to look upon all my domestic, civil, and social duties as most sacred. So help me God, both for the happiness of my life, and for the peace of my mind."

"[Initiator:] Rise, and in future beware of ever bending thy knee before him who is only man like thyself."

## Epopt (or Priest) of the Illuminati

"I. Do you think the present state of nations corresponds with the object for which man was placed upon earth?

For example, do governments, civil associations, or religion, attain the ends for which they were designed? Do the sciences to which men apply furnish them with real lights; are they conducive (as they ought to be) to real happiness? Are they not, on the contrary, the off-spring of numberless wants, and of the unnatural state in which men live? Are they not the crude inventions of crazy brains, or of geniuses laboriously subtle?"

"II. What civil associations and what sciences do you think tend or do not tend to the grand object? Did there not formerly exist an order of things more simple? What sort of an idea can you form of that ancient state of the world?"

"III. Now that we have passed through all those nullities (or through all those useless and vain forms of our civil constitutions), do you think that it would be possible to return back to the original and noble simplicity of our forefathers? Supposing we had returned to it, would not our past misfortunes render that state more durable? Would not all mankind be in a similar state with an individual who, having enjoyed the sweets of innocence during his childhood, and fallen a prey to error and his passions during his youth, at length, instructed by the risks he has run, and by experience, endeavours to return to that innocence and purity which rendered his childhood so happy?"

"IV. What means are best to be employed for restoring mankind to that happy state? Should it be by public measures, by violent revolutions, or by any means that should ensure success?"

"V. Does not the Christian Religion in all its purity afford some indications, does it not hint at some state or happiness similar to this? Does it not even prepare it?"

"VI. Is this holy and simple religion really what different Sects profess it to be at this present day, or is it more perfect?"

"VII. Can this more perfect Christianity be known or taught? Could the world (such as it now is) support a stronger degree of light? Do you not think that, before the numberless obstacles could be removed, it would be proper to preach to mankind a religion more perfect, a philosophy more elevated, and the art of each one's governing himself according to his greatest advantage?"

"VIII. Would not our moral and political views lead men to oppose this blessing? From our political and moral views then, or from an ill-judged interest, or even from deep-rooted prejudices, these obstacles originate. If men, therefore, oppose the renovation of human happiness, is it not because, slaves to ancient forms, they reject and reprobate every thing which is not to be found in those forms, though it should be the most natural, the grandest, and most noble of all possible things? Does not personal interest, alas! at present predominate over the general interest of mankind?"

"IX. Must we not then silently and gradually remedy those disorders before we can flatter ourselves with the re-establishment of the golden age? Meanwhile, is it not adviseable to disseminate the truth in Secret Societies?"

"X. Can we trace any such secret doctrine in the ancient schools of the sages, or in the allegorical lessons given by

Jesus Christ, the Saviour and liberator of mankind, to his most intimate disciples? Have you not observed a sort of gradual education in that art which you see has been transmitted to our Order, from the highest antiquity?"

"[Hierophant:]Come, enter, unhappy fugitive! The fathers wait for you; enter and shut the door after you."

[In the temple the candidate beholds a throne under a rich canopy with a table before it, on which lie a crown, a sceptre, a sword, some pieces of gold money, and precious jewels, all interlaid with chains. At the foot of this table, on a scarlet cushion, is thrown a white robe, a girdle, and the simple ornaments of a priestly costume.]

"[Hierophant:] Behold and fix thine eyes on the splendour of the throne. If all this childish mummery, these crowns, these scepters, and all these monuments of human degradation, have any charms in your eyes, speak; and it may be in our power to gratify your wishes. Unhappy man! if such are your objects, if you wish to rise to power that you may assist in the oppression of your Brethren, go, and at your peril make the trial. Are you in quest of power, of force, of false honours, and of such superfluities, we will labour for you; we will procure such transient advantages for you, we will place you as near the throne as you can desire, and will leave you to the consequences of your folly; but observe, our sanctuary shall be for ever shut against you."

"On the contrary, do you wish to be initiated into wisdom, would you teach the art of rendering men better, more free and more happy, then be welcome, be thrice welcome. Here you behold the attributes of

Royalty, and there, on the cushion, you see the modest vestment of innocence; make thy choice, and let it be the choice which thy heart shall dictate."

"[If the candidate chooses the crown] Monster, retire! cease to pollute this holy place! Begone, fly, before it is too late." [Candidate is then led out and the ritual ends]

"[But if the candidate chooses the priest raiment] Health and salutation to thy great and noble soul! Such was the choice we expected from you. But stop; it is not permitted to you to invest yourself with that robe, until you have learned to what you are in future destined by us."

"At length the time of your reward succeeds to the trials of an assiduous preparation. At present you know yourself, and have learned to know others; you are what you ought to be, such as we wished to see you. It will now be your duty to conduct others. – What you already know, and what you are about to learn, will expose to your view the extreme weakness of human nature. In this advantage alone lies the true source of power which one man exercises over another. The dark clouds dissipate; the sun of light rises; the gates of the sanctuary unfold; a portion of our mysterics is going to be revealed to you. Let the gates of the temple be shut against the prophane; I will only speak to the Illustrious, to the Holy, to the Elect. I speak to those who have ears to hear, who have tongues which they can command, and who have minds sufficiently enlightened to understand.

"Surrounded by the Illustrious, you are about to enter into that class which bears an essential part in the government of our sublime Order. But do you know what it is to govern, can you conceive what this right can be in a secret society? To exercise such an empire, not over the vulgar or the grandees of the people, but over the most accomplished men, over men in all stations, of all nations, of all religions; to reign over them without any exterior constraint, to keep them united by durable bonds, to inspire them all with one spirit; to govern with all possible precision, activity, and silence, men spread over the whole surface of the globe, even to its utmost confines. This is a problem which no political wisdom has ever been able to solve. To reunite the distinctions of Equality, Despotism, and Liberty; to prevent the treasons and persecutions which would be the inevitable consequences; of nothing, to create great things; to stand firm against the swelling torrent of evils and abuse; to make happiness universally shine on human nature; would be a master-piece of morality and polity re-united. The civil constitutions of states offer but little aid to such an undertaking. Fear and violence are their grand engines; with us, each one is voluntarily to lend his assistance. . . . Were men what they ought to be, we might on their first admission into our society explain the greatness of our plans to them; but the lure of a secret is perhaps the only means of retaining those who might turn their backs upon us as soon as their curiosity had been gratified: The ignorance or imperfect education of many makes it requisite that they should be first formed by our moral lessons. The complaints, the murmurs of others against the trials to which we are obliged to condemn them, sufficiently show you what pains we must bestow, with what patience and what constancy we must be endowed; how intensely the love of the grand object must glow in our hearts, to make us keep true to our posts in the midst of such unthankful labour; and not abandon for ever the hope of regenerating mankind."

"It is to partake with us of these labours that you have been called. To observe others day and night; to form them, to succour them, to watch over them; to stimulate the courage of the pusillanimous, the activity and the zeal of the lukewarm; to instruct the ignorant; to raise up those who have fallen, to fortify those who stagger; to repress the ardour of rashness, to prevent disunion; to veil the faults and weaknesses of others; to guard against the acute inquisitiveness of wit; to prevent imprudence and treason; in short, to maintain the subordination to and esteem of our Superiors, and friendship and union among the Brethren, are the duties, among others still greater, that we impose upon you."

"Have you any idea of secret societies; of the rank they hold, or of the parts they perform in the events of this world? Do you view them as insignificant or transient meteors? O, Brother! God and Nature, when disposing of all things according to the proper times and places, had their admirable ends in view; and they make use of these secret societies as the only and as the indispensable means of conducting us thither."

"Hearken, and may you be filled with admiration! This is the point whither all the moral tends; it is on this that depends the knowledge of the rights of secret societies, of all our doctrine, of all our ideas of good and bad, of just and unjust. You are here situated between the world past and the world to come. Cast your eyes boldly on what has passed, and in an instant ten thousand bolts shall fall, and thousands of gates shall burst open to futurity — You shall behold the inexhaustible riches of

God and of Nature, the degradation and the dignity of man. You shall see the world and human nature in its youth, if not in its childhood, even there where you thought to find it in its decrepitude and verging toward its ruin and ignominy."

"Nature makes us begin at infancy, from infancy she raises us to manhood. She at first left us in the savage state, but soon brought us to civilization, perhaps that we might be more sensible, more enraptured and tenacious of what we are, from viewing the contrast of what we were. But to what changes, and those of an order infinitely more important, does our future destiny lead us!"

"As has the individual man so human nature in the ag-gregate has its childhood, its youth, its manhood, and its old age. At each of these periods mankind learn and are subject to fresh wants--hence arise their political and moral revolutions—It is at the age of manhood that human nature appears in all its dignity. It is then that, taught by long experience, man conceives at length how great a misfortune it is for hire to invade the rights of others, to avail himself of some few advantages, purely exterior, to raise himself, to the prejudice of others. It is then that he sees and feels the happiness and dignity of man."

"The first age of mankind is that of savage and uncouth nature. A family is the whole society; hunger and thirst easily quenched, a shelter from the inclemency of the seasons, a woman, and, after fatigue, rest, are then the only wants. At that period men enjoyed the two most inestimable blessings Equality and Liberty; they enjoyed them to their utmost extent; they would have forever enjoyed them, had they chosen to follow the track which Nature had traced for them — or had it not entered the plans of God and Nature first to show man for what happiness he was destined; happiness the more precious, as he had begun by tasting it; happiness so early lost, but instantaneously regretted and fruitlessly sought after, until he should have learned how to make proper use of his strength, and how to conduct himself in his intercourse with the rest of mankind. In his primitive state he was destitute of the conveniencies of life, but he was not on that account unhappy; not knowing them, he did not feel the want of them. Health was his ordinary state, and physical pain was his only source of uneasiness — Oh happy mortals! who were not sufficiently enlightened to disturb the repose of your mind, or to feel those great agents of our miseries the love of power and of distinctions, the propensity to sensuality, the thirst after the representative signs of all wealth, those truly original sins with all their progeny, envy, avarice, intemperance, sickness, and all the tortures of imagination!"

"An infortunate germ soon vivifies in the breast of man, and his primitive peace and felicity disappear."

"As families multiplied, the means of subsistence began to fail; the nomade (or roaming) life ceased, and property started into existence; men chose habitations; agriculture made them intermix. Language became universal; living together, one man began to measure his strength with another, and the weaker were distinguished from the stronger. This undoubtedly created the idea of mutual defence, of one individual governing divers families reunited, and of thus defending their persons and their fields against the invasion of an enemy; but hence Liberty was ruined in its foundation, and Equality disappeared."

"Oppressed with wants unknown until that period, man perceived that his own powers were no longer sufficient. To supply this defect, the weakest imprudently submitted to the strongest or to the wisest; not however to be ill-treated, but that he might be protected, conducted, and enlightened. — All submission, therefore, even of the most unpolished mortal, has an existence only in as much as he wants the person to whom he subjects himself, and on the express condition that that person can succour him. His power ceases when my weakness no longer exists, or when another acquires superiority. Kings are fathers; the paternal power is at an end when the child has acquired his strength. The father would offend his children if he pretended to prolong his rights beyond that term. Every man having attained to years of discretion may govern himself, when a whole nation therefore is arrived at that period, there can exist no further plea for keeping it in wardship. "

"You who thus give oracles, what do you understand by nations having attained their majority? Without doubt such as, having emerged from ignorance and barbarism, have acquired the lights necesssary for their happiness; and to what can they be indebted for these lights and this happiness, if not to their civil association? It will be then, if ever, that they will find it both reasonable and necessary to remain under the guardianship of their laws and of their government, lest they should fall back into the barbarism and ignorance of the roaming clans, or be precipitated into the horrors of anarchy, from revolution to revolution, under the successive tyranny of the brigand, of the executioner of the sophisticated despot, or under that of a sophister Syeyes and his colegislative Marsellois, of a Robespierre and his guillotines, of the Triumvirs and their proscriptions. The populace alone in the minority of ignorance, the sophisters alone in the majority of wickedness and corruption, shall applaud thy mysteries."

"Never did strength submit to weakness. — Nature has destined the weak to serve, because they have wants; the strong man to govern, because he can be useful. Let the one lose his force, and the other acquire it, they will then change situations, and he that obeyed will command. He that stands in need of another, also depends upon him, and he has renounced to him his rights. Hence few wants is the first step towards liberty. It is for this reason that the savages are the most enlightened of men, and perhaps they alone are free. 9 When wants are durable, servitude is also lasting. Safety is a durable want. Had men refrained from all injustice, they would have remained free; it was injustice which made them bend beneath the yoke. To acquire safety, they deposited the whole force in the hands of one man; and thus created a new evil, that of fear. The work of their own hands frightened them; and to live in safety they robbed themselves of that very safety. This is the cause of our governments. — Where then shall we find a protecting force? In union; but how rare, alas! is that union, except in our new and secret associations, better guided by wisdom, and leagued in straiter bonds! and hence it is that nature itself inclines us toward these associations."

"Such is the faithful and philosophic picture of despotism and of liberty, of our wishes and of our fears. Despotism was engrafted on liberty, and from despotism shall liberty once more spring. The re-union of men in society is at once the cradle and the grave of despotism; it is also the grave and cradle of liberty. We were once possessed of liberty, and we lost it but to find it again and never lose it more; to learn by the very privation of it the art of better enjoying it in future."

"Nature drew men from the savage state and re-united them in civil societies; from these societies we proceed to further wishes, and to a wiser choice (aus den staaten tretten wir in neue klüger gewählte). New associations present themselves to these wishes, and by their means we return to the state whence we came, not again to run the former course, but better to enjoy our new destiny — let us explain this mystery."

"Men then had passed from their peaceable state to the yoke of servitude; Eden, that terrestrial paradise, was lost to them. Subjects of sin and slavery, they were reduced to servitude and obliged to gain their bread by the sweat of their brow. — In the number of these men some promised to protect, and thus became their chiefs — at first they reigned over herds or clans — these were soon conquered, or united together in order to form a numerous people; hence arose nations and their chiefs kings of nations. At the formation of states and nations, the world ceased to be a great family, to be a single empire; the great bond of nature was rent asunder."

"[When nations formed] they ceased to acknowledge a common name — Nationalism, or the love for a particular nation, took place of the general love. With the division of the globe, and of its states, benevolence was restrained within certain limits, beyond which it could no longer trespass. — Then it became a merit to extend the bounds of states at the expence of the neighbouring ones. Then it became lawful to abuse, offend, and despise foreigners, to attain that end—and this virtue was styled patriotism; and he was styled a patriot who, just toward his countrymen, and unjust to others, was blind to the merits of strangers, and believed the very vices of his own country to be perfections.—In such a case, why not restrain that love within a narrower compass, to citizens living in the same town, or to the members of one family; or why even should not each person have concentrated his affections in himself. We really beheld Patriotism generating Localism, the confined spirit of families, and at length Egoism. Hence the origin of states and governments, and of civil society, has really proved to be the seeds of discord, and Patriotism has found its punishment in itself . . .Diminish, reject that love of the country, and mankind will once more learn to know and love each other as men. Partiality being cast aside, that union of hearts will once more appear and expand itself—on the contrary, extend the bonds of Patriotism, and you will teach man that it is impossible to blame the closer contraction of love, to a single family, to a single person, in a word, to the strictest Egoism."

"Oh nature! How great and incontestible are thy rights? It is from the womb of disaster and mutual destruction that the means of safety spring! Oppression disappears because it meets with abettors, and reason regains its rights because people wish to stifle it. He, at least, who wishes to mislead others, should seek to govern them by the advantages of instruction and science. Kings themselves at length perceive, that there is little glory in reigning over ignorant herds—Legislators begin to acquire wisdom, and they favour property and industry:—perverse motives propagate the sciences, and Kings protect them as agents of oppression. Other men profit of them to investigate the origin of their rights. They at length seize on that unknown mean of forwarding a revolution in the human mind, and of thus triumphing for ever over oppression. But the triumph would be of short duration, and man would fall back into his degraded state, had not Providence in those distant ages husbanded the means which it has transmitted down to us, of secretly meditating and at length operating the salvation of human kind.

"Those means are, the secret schools of Philosophy. Those schools have been in all ages the archives of nature and of the rights of man. These schools shall one day retrieve the fall of human nature, and Princes and Nations shall disappear from the face of the earth, and that without any violence. Human nature shall form one great family, and the earth shall become the habitation of the man of reason.—Morality shall alone produce this great Revolution. The day shall come when each father shall, like Abraham and the Patriarchs, become the Priest and absolute Sovereign of his family. Reason shall be the only book of laws, the sole Code of man. This is one of our grand mysteries. Attend to the demonstration of it, and learn how it has been transmitted down to us."

"What strange blindness can have induced men to imagine that human nature was always to be governed as it has hitherto been.

"Where shall we find a man acquainted with all the resources of nature? Who dare prescribe limits, and say thus far shalt thou proceed, and no farther, to that nature, whose law is unity in the variegated infinite?

Whence shall issue the command, that it shall always run the same course, and for ever renew it again— Where is the being who has condemned men, the best, the wisest, and the most enlightened of men, to perpetual slavery? Why should human nature be bereft of its most perfect attribute, that of governing itself? Why are those persons to be always led who are capable of conducting themselves? Is it then impossible for mankind or at least the greater part, to come to their majority? If one be enabled to do it why should not another; show to one person what you have taught another; teach him the grand art of mastering his passions and regulating his desires; teach him, that from his earliest youth he stands in need of others; that he must abstain from giving offence if he wishes not to be offended; that he must be beneficent if he wishes to receive favours. Let him be patient, indulgent, wise, and benevolent. Let these virtues be made easy to him by principles, experience, and examples; and you will soon see whether he needs another to conduct him? If it be true, that the greater part of mankind are too weak or too ignorant to conceive these simple truths, and to be convinced by them; Oh then our happiness will be at an end, and let us cease to labour at rendering mankind better, or at seeking to enlighten them."

"Oh prejudice! oh contradiction of the human mind! shall the empire of reason, the capacity of governing ourselves, be but a chimerical dream for the greater number of men, while on the other hand prejudice leads us to believe that such is the inherent right of the children of Kings, of reigning families, and of every man whom wisdom or particular circumstances render independent!"

"Are we then fallen from our dignity so low as not even to feel our chains, or to hug them, and not cherish the flattering hope of being able to break them, or to recover our liberty, not by rebellion or violence (for the time is not yet come), but by force of reason. Because a thing cannot be accomplished to-morrow, should we despair of ever being able to effect it? Abandon such short-sighted men to their own reasonings and their own conclusions; they may conclude again and again; but nature will continue to act. Inexorable to all their interested remonstrances, she proceeds, and nothing can impede her majestic course. Some events may take place contrary to our wishes; but they will all rectify of themselves; inequalities will be levelled, and a lasting calm shall succeed the tempest. The only conclusion to be drawn from all these objections is, that we are too much accustomed to the present state of things, or perhaps self-interest has too great sway over us, to let us own that it is not impossible to attain universal independence— Let then the laughers laugh and the scoffers scoff. He that observes and compares what Nature has done with what she does at present, will soon see, that in spite of all our intrigues she tends invariably toward her object. Her proceedings are imperceptible to him who reflects but little; they are visible only to the sage whose mind's eye penetrates even to the womb of time.—From the summit of the mount he discovers in the horizon that distant country, the very existence of which is not surmised by the servile multitude of the plain."

"He on the contrary who wishes to render mankind free, teaches them how to refrain from the acquisition of things which they cannot afford: he enlightens them, he infuses into them boldness and inflexible manners. He that teaches them sobriety, temperance, and œconomy, is more dangerous to the throne than the man who openly preaches regicide. — If you cannot diffuse at the same instant this degree of light among all men, at least begin by enlightening yourself, and by rendering yourself better. Serve, assist, and mutually support each other; augment our numbers; render yourselves at least independent, and leave to time and posterity the care of doing the rest. When your numbers shall be augmented to a certain degree, when you shall have acquired strength by your union, hesitate no longer, but begin to render yourself powerful and formidable to the wicked (that is to say to all who will resist their plans); the very circumstance of your being sufficiently numerous to talk of force, and that you really do talk of it, that circumstance alone makes the prophane and wicked tremble — That they may not be overpowered by numbers, many will become good (like you) of themselves, and will join your party. — You will soon acquire sufficient force to bind the hands of your opponents, to subjugate them and to stifle wickedness in the embryo." That is to say, as it may be understood in future, you will soon be able to stifle every principle of law, of government, of civil or political society, whose very institution in the eyes of an Illuminee is the germ of all the vices and misfortunes of human nature. "The mode of diffusing universal light, is not to proclaim it at once to the whole world, but to begin with yourself; then turn toward your next neighbour; you two can enlighten a third and fourth; let these in the same manner extend and multiply the number of the children of light, until numbers and force shall throw power into our hands."

"Let your instructions and lights be universally diffused; so shall you render mutual security universal; and security and instruction will enable us to live without prince or government. If that were not the case, why should we go in quest of either?"

"For if light be the work of morality, light and security will gain strength as morality expands itself. Nor is true morality any other than the art of teaching men to shake off their wardship, to attain the age of manhood, and thus to need neither princes nor governments."

"He is little acquainted with the powers of reason and the attractions of virtue; he is a very novice in the regions of light, who shall harbour such mean ideas as to his own essence, or the nature of mankind... If either he or I can attain this point, why should not another attain it also? What! when men can be led to despise the horrors of death, when they may be inflamed with the enthusiasm of religious and political follies, shall they be deaf to that very doctrine which can alone lead them to happiness? No, no; man is not so wicked as an arbitrary morality would make him appear. He is wicked, because Religion, the State, and bad example, perverts him. It would be of advantage to those who wish to make him better, were there fewer persons whose interest it is to render him wicked in order that they may support their power by his wickedness."

"Let us form a more liberal opinion of human nature. We will labour indefatigably, nor shall difficulties affright us. May our principles become the foundation of all morals! Let reason at length be the religion of men, and the problem is solved."

"Since such is the force of morality and of morality alone, since it alone can operate the grand revolution which is to restore liberty to mankind, and abolish the empire of imposture, superstition, and despotism; you must now perceive why on their first entrance into our Order we oblige our pupils to apply closely to the study of morality, to the knowledge of themselves and of others. You must see plainly, that if we permit each Novice to introduce his friend, it is in order to form a legion that may more justly he called holy and invincible than that of the Theban; since the battles of the friend fighting by the side of his friend are those which are to reinstate human nature in its rights, its liberty, and its primitive independence."

"The morality which is to perform this miracle is not a morality of vain subtleties. It is not that morality which, degrading man, renders him careless of the goods of this world, forbids him the enjoyment of the innocent pleasures of life, and inspires him with the hatred of his neighbour. It must not be a morality favouring the interests only of its teachers, which prescribes persecution and intoleration, which militates against reason, which forbids the prudent use of the passions; whose virtues are no other than inaction, idleness, and the heaping of riches on the slothful. — Above all, it must not be that morality which, adding to the miseries of the miserable, throws them into a state of pusillanimity and despair, by the threats of hell and the fear of devils.

"It must, on the contrary, be that morality so much disregarded and defaced at the present day by selfishness, and replete with heterogeneous principles. It must be a divine doctrine, such as Jesus taught to his disciples, and of which he gave the real interpretation in his secret conferences."

"[The] grand and ever-celebrated master, Jesus of Nazareth, appeared in an age when corruption was universal; in the midst of a people who from time immemorial had been subjected to, and severely felt the yoke of slavery; and who eagerly expected their deliverer announced by the Prophets. Jesus appeared and taught the doctrine of reason; to give greater efficacy to these doctrines, he formed them into a religion, and adopted the received traditions of the Jews. He prudently grafted his new school on their religion and their customs, which he made the vehicle of the essence and secrets of his new doctrines. He did not select sages for his new disciples, but ignorant men chosen from the lowest class of the people, to show that his doctrine was made for all, and suitable to every one's understanding; to show too, that the knowledge of the grand truths of reason was not a privilege peculiar to the great. He does not teach the Jews alone, but all mankind, the means of acquiring their liberty, by the observation of his precepts. He supported his doctrines by an innocent life, and sealed them with his blood."

"His precepts for the salvation of the world are, simply, the love of God and the love of our neighbour; he asks no more... Nobody ever reduced and consolidated the bonds of human society within their real limits as he did — No one was ever more intelligible to his hearers, or more prudently covered the sublime signification of his doctrine. No one, indeed, ever laid a surer foundation for liberty than our grand master, Jesus of Nazareth. It is true, that on all occasions he carefully concealed the sublime meaning and natural consequences of his doctrines; for he had a secret doctrine, as is evident from more than one passage of the Gospel."

"To you is given to know the mystery of the kingdom of God; but to them that are without, all things are done in parables."

"And their princes have power over them but it is not so among you; but whoever will be greater shall be your minister."

"If therefore the object of the secret of Jesus, which has been preserved by the institution of the mysteries, and clearly demonstrated both by the conduct and the discourses of this divine master, was to reinstate mankind in their original Equality and Liberty, and to prepare the means; how many things immediately appear clear and natural, which hitherto seemed to be contradictory and unintelligible! This explains in what sense Christ was the saviour and the liberator of the world. Now the doctrine of original sin, of the fall of man, and of his regeneration, can be understood. The state of pure nature, of fallen or corrupt nature, and the state of grace, will no longer be a problem. Mankind, in quitting their state of original liberty, fell from the state of nature and lost their dignity. In their civil society, under their governments, they no longer live in the state of pure nature, but in that of fallen and corrupt nature. If the moderating of their passions and the diminution of their wants, reinstate them in their primitive dignity, that will really constitute their redemption and their state of grace. It is to this point that morality, and the most perfect of all morality, that of Jesus, leads mankind. When at length this doctrine shall be generalized throughout the world, the reign of the good and of the elect shall be established."

"The Freemasons, like Priests and chiefs of nations, have banished reason from the earth. They have inundated the world with tyrants, impostors, spectres, corpses, and men like to wild beasts."

"Though these mysterious Associations should not attain our object, they prepare the way for us; they give a new interest to the cause; they present it under points of view hitherto unobserved; they stimulate the inventive powers and the expectations of mankind; they render men more indifferent as to the interests of governments; they bring men of divers nations and religions within the same bond of union; they deprive the church and the state of their ablest and most laborious members; they bring men together who would never otherwise have known or met each other. By this method alone they undermine the foundation of states, though they had really no such project in view. They throw them together and make them clash one against the other. They teach mankind the power and force of union; they point out to them the imperfection of their political constitutions, and that without exposing them to the suspicions of their enemies, such as magistrates and public governments. They mask our progress, and procure us the facility of incorporating in our plans and of admitting into our Order, after the proper trials, the most able men, whose patience, long abused, thirsts after the grand ultimatum. By this means they weaken the enemy; and though they should never triumph over him, they will at least diminish the numbers and the zeal of his partizans; they divide his troops to cover the attack. In proportion as these new associations or secret societies, formed in different states, shall acquire strength and prudence at the expence of the former ones (that is to say, of civil society), the latter must weaken, and insensibly fall."

"Beside, our Society originates, and must naturally and essentially deduce its origin from those very governments whose vices have rendered our union necessary. We have no object but that better order of things for which we incessantly labour; all the efforts, therefore, of Princes to stop our progress will be fruitless; the spark may long remain hidden in the ashes, but the day must come in which shall burst forth the general flame. For nature nauseates always to run the same course. The heavier the yoke of oppression weighs on man, the more sedulously will he labour to throw it off; and the liberty he seeks shall expand itself. The seed is sown whence shall spring a new world; the roots extend themselves; they have acquired too much strength, they have been too industriously propagated, for the day of harvest to fail us. — Perhaps it may be necessary to wait thousands and thousands of years; but sooner or later nature shall consummate its grand work, and she shall restore that dignity to man for which he was destined from the beginning."

"We are here at once the observers and the instruments of nature. — We do not wish to precipitate her steps. To enlighten men, to correct their morals, to inspire them with benevolence, such are our means. Secure of success, we abstain from violent commotions. To have foreseen the happiness of posterity, and to have prepared it by irreproachable means, suffices for our felicity. The tranquility of our consciences is not troubled by the reproach of aiming at the ruin or overthrow of states and thrones. Such an accusation could with no more propriety be preferred against us, than it might against

234 NEW HERMETICS EQUINOX JOURNAL VOLUME 3

the statesmen who had foreseen and foretold the impending and inevitable ruin of the state.—As assiduous observers of Nature, we admire her majestic course; and, burning with the noble pride of our origin, we felicitate ourselves on being the children of men and of God."

"But carefully observe and remember, that we do not impose our opinions; we do not oblige you to adopt our doctrines. Let the truth you can acknowledge be your only guide. Free man, exercise here thy primitive right; seek, doubt, examine; do you know of, or can you find elsewhere, any thing that is better?—Make us acquainted with your views, as we have exposed ours to you. We do not blush at the limits of our understandings; we know that we are but men; we know that such are the dispositions of nature, such the lot of man, that he is not to expect to attain perfection at his outset; he can attain it but by degrees. It is by gaining experience from our errors, by profiting of the lights acquired by our forefathers, that we shall become at once the children of wisdom, and the parents of a still wiser progeny. If, therefore, you think that you have found truth in the whole of our doctrine, adopt the whole. Should you perceive any error to have stolen in with it, remember that truth is not the less estimable on that account. If you have met with nothing that pleases you here, reject the whole without fear; and remember, that in many things, at least, we only need further research, or a new investigation. Do you observe any thing blameable or laudable, see and make choice of what you approve. Should you be more enlightened yourself, then your eye may have discovered truths which are still denied to us. The more art we employ in the instruction of our pupils to lead them to the paths of wisdom, the less you will be inclined to refuse us a portion of your applause."

"[not sure where these next two fit so I'm just putting then at the end] Nature, which had preserved the true race of men in its original vigour and purity, came to the assistance of mankind. From distant, but poor and sterile countries, she calls those savage nations and sends them into the regions of luxury and voluptuousness to infuse new life into the enervated species of the south; and with new laws and morals to restore that vigour to human nature which flourished until an ill-extinguished germ of corruption infected even that portion of mankind which originally arrived in so pure a state"

"Oh had there remained any sages among them, happy enough to have preserved themselves from the contagion, how would they sigh after, and ardently wish to return to the former abodes of their ancestors, there again to enjoy their former pleasures on the banks of a rivulet, under the shade of a tree laden with fruit, by the side of the object of their affections! It was then that they conceived the high value of Liberty, and the greatness of the fault they had committed in placing too much power in the hands of one man—It was then that the want of Liberty made them sensible of their fall, and seek means of softening the rigour of Slavery;—but even then their efforts were only aimed against the tyrant, and not against tyranny."

[the candidate is eventually given a robe and red cap and given milk and honey as a sacrament]

## Regent (Prince) of the Illuminati

"I. Would you think a society objectionable, which should (till nature shall have ripened its grand revolutions) place itself in a situation, that would deprive Monarchs of the power of doing harm, though they should wish it; a society whose invisible means should prevent all governments from abusing their power? Would it be impossible, through the influence of such a society, to form a new state in each state, status in statu;" that is to say, would it be impossible to subject the rulers of every state to this Illuminizing Society, and to convert them into mere tools of the Order even in the government of their own dominions?

"II. Were it to be objected, that such a society would abuse its power, would not the following considerations do away such an objection? — Do not our present rulers daily abuse their power? And are not the people silent, notwithstanding such an abuse? Is this power as secure from abuse in the hands of Princes, as it would be in those of our adepts whom we train up with so much care? If then any government could be harmless, would it not be our's, which would be entirely founded on morality, foresight, wisdom, liberty, and virtue?"

"III. Though this universal government, founded on morality, should prove chimerical, would it not be worth while to make an essay of it?"

"IV. Would not the most sceptical man find a sufficient guarantee against any abuse of power on the part of our Order, in the liberty of abandoning it at pleasure; in the happiness of having Superiors of tried merit, who, unknown to each other, could not possibly support each other in their treasonable combinations against the general welfare; Superiors, in short, who would be deterred from doing harm by the fear of the existing chiefs of empires?"

"V. Should there exist any other secret means of guarding against the abuse of that authority entrusted by the order to our Superiors, what might they be?"

"VI. Supposing despotism were to ensure, would it be dangerous in the hands of men who, from the very first step we made in the Order, teach us nothing but science, liberty, and virtue? Would not that despotism lose its sting, in the consideration that those chiefs who may have conceived dangerous plans will have begun by disposing a machine in direct opposition to their views."

"Provincial. Who brought this slave to us?"

"Introducer. He came of his own accord; he knocked at the door."

"Prov. What does he want?"

"Introd. He is in search of Liberty, and asks to be freed from his chains."

"Prov. Why does he not apply to those who have chained him?"

"Introd. They refuse to break his bonds; they acquire too great an advantage from his slavery."

"Prov. Who then is it that has reduced him to this state of slavery?"

"Introd. Society, governments, the sciences, and false religion."

"Prov. And he wishes to cast off this yoke to become a seditious man and a rebel?"

"Introd. No; he wishes to unite with us, to join in our fights against the constitution of governments, the corruption of morals, and the profanation of religion. He wishes through our means to become powerful, that he may attain the grand ultimatum."

"Prov. And who will answer to us, that after having obtained that power he will not also abuse it, that he will not be a tyrant and the author of new misfortunes?"

"Introd. His heart and his reason are our guarantees— the Order has enlightened him. He has learned to conquer his passions and to know himself. Our Superiors have tried him."

"Prov. That is saying a great deal—Is he also superior to prejudice. Does he prefer the general interest of the universe to that of more limited associations?"

"Introd. Such have been his promises."

"Prov. How many others have made similar promises who did not keep them? Is he master of himself? Can he resist temptation? Are personal considerations of no avail with respect to him? Ask him, whether the skeleton he has before him is that of a king, a nobleman, or a beggar?"

"Introd. He cannot tell; nature has destroyed all that marked the depraved state of inequality; all that he sees is, that this skeleton was man like us; and the character of man is all that he attends to."

"Prov. If such be his sentiments, let him be free at his own risk and peril. But he knows us not. Go and ask him why he implores our protection?

"Brother, the knowledge you have acquired can no longer leave you in doubt as to the grandeur, the importance, the disinterestedness and lawfulness of our great object. It must therefore be indifferent to you whether you are acquainted with our Superiors or not; nevertheless, I have some information to impart to you on that subject."

"When questioned as to whom we are indebted to for the actual constitution of our Order, and the present form of the inferior degrees, the following is the answer we give:

"Our founders, without doubt, had extensive knowledge, since they have transmitted so much to us. — Actuated by a laudable zeal for the general welfare, they formed a code of laws for our Order; but, partly through prudence, and partly to guard against their own passions, they left the direction of the edifice they had raised to other hands, and retired. Their names will for ever remain in oblivion — The chiefs who govern the Order at present are not our founders; but posterity will doubly bless those unknown benefactors who have despised the vain glory of immortalizing their names. Every document which could have thrown light on our origin has been committed to the flames."

"You will now be under the direction of other men; men who, gradually educated by the Order, have at length been placed at the helm. You will soon make one of their number—Tell me only, whether you still harbour any doubt as to the object of the Order."

"Prov. Wretch! You are a slave: and yet dare enter an assembly of free men! Do you know the fate that awaits you? You have passed through two doors to enter this; but you shall not go hence unpunished, if you prophane this sanctuary."

"Introd. That will not happen; I will be his guarantee. You have taught him to thirst after liberty; and now keep your promise."

"Prov. Well, Brother, we have subjected you to various trials. The elevation of your sentiments has made us conceive you to be both proper and worthy of being admitted into our Order. You have thrown yourself with confidence and without reserve into our arms: and it is time to impart to you that liberty which we have painted to you in such bewitching colours. We have been your guide during all the time that you stood in need of one. You are now strong enough to conduct yourself, be then in future your own guide, be it at your own peril and risk. Be free; that is to say, be a man, and a man who knows how to govern himself, a man who knows his duty, and his imprescriptible rights; a man who serves the universe alone; whose actions are solely directed to the general benefit of the world and of human nature. Every thing else is injustice—Be free and independent; in future be so of yourself.—Here, take back the engagements you have hitherto contracted with us. To you we return them all."

[all papers, oaths, diaries etc. that were collected throughout the candidate's association with the Illuminati are returned to him]

"In future you will owe us nothing but that which your heart shall dictate. We do not tyrannize over men, we only enlighten them. Have you found contentment, rest, satisfaction, happiness, among us? You will not then abandon us. Can we have mistaken you, or can you have mistaken us! It would be a misfortune for you; but you are free. Remember only that men free and independent do not offend each other; on the contrary, they assist and mutually protect each other. Remember, that to offend another man, is to give him the right of defending himself. Do you wish to make a noble use of the power we give to you? rely on our word: you shall find zeal and protection among us. Could a disinterested zeal for your brethren glow in your heart, then labour at the grand object, labour for unfortunate human nature, and thy last hour shall be blest. We ask nothing else from you, we ask nothing for ourselves. Question your own heart, and let it say whether our conduct to you has not been noble and disinterested. After so many favours, could you be ungrateful, your heart should avenge us, and chastise you. But no; many trials have proved you to be man of constancy and resolution. Be such your character, and in future govern with us oppressed man, and labour at rendering him virtuous and free."

"Oh, Brother! what a fight, what hopes! when one day happiness, affection, and peace shall be the inhabitants of the earth! when misery, error, and oppression, shall disappear with superfluous wants! when, each one at his station labouring only for the general good, every father of a family shall be sovereign in his tranquil cot! when he that wishes to invade these sacred rights shall not find an asylum on the face of the earth! when idleness shall be no longer suffered! when the clod of useless sciences shall be cast aside, and none shall be taught but those which contribute to make man better, and to reinstate him in his primitive freedom, his future destiny! when we may flatter ourselves with having forwarded that happy period, and complacently view the fruits of our labours! when, in fine, each man viewing his brother in his fellow-creature, shall extend a succouring hand—with us and ours you shall find happiness and peace, should you continue faithful and attached to us. You will also remark, that the sign of this degree consists in extending your arms to a brother with your hands open, to show that they are not sullied by injustice and oppression, and the gripe is to seize the brother by the two elbows, as it were to hinder him from falling. The word is redemption."

[the candidate is presented with a buckler, boots, a cloak, and a hat].

On presenting the buckler, the Initiator says, "Arm thyself with fidelity, truth, and constancy; be a true Christian, and the shafts of calumny and misfortune shall not pierce thee."

On presenting the boots: "Be active in the service of the good, and fear no road which may lead to the propagation or discovery of happiness."

On giving the cloak: "Be a prince over thy people; that is to say, be sincere and wise, the benefactor of thy brethren, and teach them science."

The formula of the hat is, "Beware of ever exchanging this hat of liberty for a crown."

# Instruction A.
## Plan of the General Government of the Order

"I. The most high and excellent Superiors of the illustrious Order of true Freemasonry do not immediately attend to the minutiæ of the edifice. — They must not, however, on that account be considered as contributing less to our happiness, by their counsels, their lessons, their plans, and the many and powerful resources with which they furnish us.

"II. These excellent and most gracious Superiors have established a class of Masons to whom they have entrusted the whole plan of our Order. This class is that of the Regents. . .

"III. In this plan our Regents hold the first dignities. Until admitted to this degree, no person can hold the office of Prefect or of Local Superior.

"IV. Every country has its national Superior, who holds an immediate correspondence with our Fathers, at the head of whom is a General who holds the helm of the Order.

"V. Under the National and his Assistants are the Provincials, who each govern their Circle or their Province.

"VI. Every Provincial is surrounded by his Counsellors.

"VII. Each Provincial also commands a certain number of Prefects, who may in like manner have their coadjutors in their districts. All these, as well as the Dean, belong to the class of Regents.

"VIII. All these offices are for life, excepting in cases of deposition or ejectment.

"IX. The Provincial is to be chosen by the Regents of his province and the National Superiors, and approved by the National.

"X. The whole success of Illuminism depending on the Regents, it is but just that their domestic wants should be provided for. They shall therefore be the first supplied from out of the funds of the Order.

"XI. The Regents of each Province form a particular body immediately under the Provincial, whom they are to obey......

"XII. The offices of Illuminism not being considered in the light of dignities, nor of places of honour, but as mere employments freely accepted, the Regents must be always ready to labour for the good of the Order, each according to his situation and to his talents. Age is never to be set forth as a title. It may often happen, that the youngest is chosen Provincial, and the eldest only a Local Superior or Counsellor, should the one live in the center, while the other only inhabits the extremity of the Province; or, should the former, on account of his natural activity or his station in life, be more fitted for the place of Superior than the latter, though far more eloquent. In many cases, for example, a Regent is not to think it beneath his dignity to offer himself to discharge any of the lesser offices in the Minerval churches (lodges) in which he may be useful.

"XIII. That the Provincial may not be overburdened with too extensive a correspondence, all the Quibus Licets, and all the letters of the Regents, shall pass through the hands of the Prefect, unless the Provincial gives Orders to the contrary.

"XIV. But the Prefect shall not open the letters of the Regents. Those he must transmit to the Provincial, who will forward them to their proper destination.

"XV. The Provincial has the power of convoking the whole of his Regents, or merely those whom he may think proper, considering the exigencies of the Province. He who cannot attend according to his summons must give the proper notice at least four weeks prior to the meeting. Beside, he is always to be ready to give in an account of what he has done for the Order until that period, and show willingness to fulfil the intentions of his Provincial and of his high Superiors. The convocation of Regents must take place at least once a year.

"XVI. The following instruction (B) will point out more particularly to the Regents those objects to which they must chiefly attend.

"XVII. It has been already observed, that great attention is to be paid to the gradually procuring of funds for the Order. This may be accomplished by attending to the following rules:

"Each province is to be entrusted with the expenditure of its own monies, and only remit small contributions to the Superiors for the expences of postage. Each Lodge also is to enjoy the full propriety of its funds — when for any great enterprize the assembly of the Regents levy contributions on the funds of the different Lodges, they shall be considered but as loans, and shall be made good to the Lodges with full interest."

"The Provincial has no fund allotted to him, but he has an exact return of all those of his province."

"The general receipts will consist—1°. In the contributions paid on the receptions of Masons —2°. In the over-plus of the monthly contributions—3°. In voluntary subscriptions—4°. In fines—5°. In legacies and donations—6°. In our commerce and traffic."

"The expenses are—1°. The expenses of the meetings, postage, decorations, and some few journeys—2°. Pensions to the poor brethren who have no other means of subsistence—3°. Sums paid for the promotion of the grand object of the Order—4°. Sums paid for the encouraging of talents—5°. The expenses of experiments and trials—6°. For widows and children—7°. For foundations."

# Instruction B
# For the Whole Degree of Regent

"I. The object of the Order being to render man more happy, virtue more attractive, and vice less powerful, it is necesssary that our brethren, the teachers and governors of mankind, should publicly assume an unimpeachable character. A Regent of Illuminism therefore will be the most perfect of men. He will be prudent, provident, ingenious, irreproachable, and of manners so urbane that his company shall be courted with avidity. He is to acquire the reputation of being enlightened, benevolent, honest, disinterested, and full of ardour for great and extraordinary enterprises, all contributing to the general good."

"II. The Regents are to study the means of ruling and governing without betraying any such intention. Under the mask of humility, but of a real and candid humility, grounded on the persuasion of their own weakness, and on the conviction that their whole strength rests on our union, they must exercise an absolute and boundless dominion, and must direct every thing toward the attainment of the views of the Order."

"Let them avoid a pedantic reserve, at once disgusting and ridiculous in the eyes of the sage. Let them give the example of a respectful submission to the Superiors. Should they be possessed of the advantages of birth, it will be an additional reason for showing their obedience to a Superior born in a lower station of life—Let their conduct vary according to the persons with whom they have to deal. Let the Regent be the confidant of one, the father of another, the scholar of a third; very seldom a severe and inexorable Superior, and even on such occasions let him show with how much unwillingness he exercises such severity. He will say, for example, that he sincerely wishes the Order had given so disagreeable a commission to some other person; and that he is weary of acting the part of schoolmaster with a man who should long since have known how to conduct himself."

"III. The grand object of our sacred legions spread throughout the universe being the triumph of virtue and of wisdom, every Regent must endeavour to establish a certain equality among men. — Let him take the part of those who are too much debased, and humble the proud. Let him never suffer the fool to lord it too much over the man of wit, the wicked over the good, the ignorant over the learned, nor the weak over the strong, though the latter should in reality be in the wrong.

"IV. The means of acquiring an ascendancy over men are incalculable. Who could enumerate them all?. They must vary with the disposition of the dines. At one period it is a taste for the marvellous and extraordinary that is to be wrought upon. At another the lure of secret societies is to be held out. "For this reason it is very proper to make your inferiors believe, without telling them the real state of the case, that all other secret societies, particularly that of Freemasonry, are secretly directed by us. Or else, and it is really the fact in some states, that potent Monarchs are governed by our Order. When any thing remarkable or important comes to pass, hint that it originated with our Order. — Should any person by his merit acquire a great reputation, let it be generally understood that he is one of us."

"With no other object than to give your orders the appearance of coming from a mysterious hand, you may, for example, put a letter under the plate of an adept when dining at an inn, though it might have been a much less trouble to forward it to him at his own lodgings — You may attend large and commercial towns during the time of fairs in different characters, as a Merchant, an Officer, an Abbé. Every where you will personate an extraordinary man having important business on your hands. — But all this must be done with a great deal of art and caution, lest you should have the appearance of an adventurer. It is to be well understood, that these characters are not to be assumed in towns where you are likely to be discovered either by the Police or the standers-by. — At other times, you may write your orders with a chemical preparation of ink, which disappears after a certain time.

"V. A Regent is as much as possible to hide from his inferiors all his weaknesses, even his ill-health, or disgusts; at any rate, he is never to complain.

"VI. Here he repeats the instruction on the art of flattering and gaining over women to their cause, already transcribed, page 43.

"VII. You must also gain over to the Order the common people. The great plan for succeeding in this is to influence the Schools. You may also attempt it by liberalities, or by great show and splendour; at other times by making yourself popular, and even tolerating, with an air of patience, prejudices which may hereafter be gradually eradicated.

"VIII. When you have succeeded any where in making yourself master of the public authority and government, you will pretend not to have the least power, for fear of awakening the attention of those who may oppose us. But, on the contrary, when you find it impossible to succeed, you will assume the character of a person who has every thing at his command. That will make us both feared and sought after, and of course will strengthen our party.

"IX. All the ill success or disgusts which may befall the Order are to be concealed with the utmost caution from the inferiors."

"X. It is the duty of the Regents to supply the wants of the Brethren, and to procure the best employments for them, after having given the proper intimation to the Superior."

"XI. The Regents shall be particularly cautious and discreet in their discourse; — but shall carefully avoid any thing denoting the least perplexity of mind — There are even some occasions whereon an extensive genius is to be affected; on others, they may pretend that their friendship has made them say a word too much; by these means the secrecy of the inferior is put to the test. They may also spread certain reports among our people, which may prepare them to receive ideas which the Order wishes to infuse into their minds. On all doubtful occasions, the Regent will consult his Superiors by means of a Quibus Licet."

"XII. Whatever rank or station a Regent may hold in the Order, he will seldom answer the questions of the inferiors verbally, but generally in writing, that he may have time to reflect or even consult on the answers he should give."

"XIII. The Regents will unceasingly attend to every thing relating to the grand interests of the Order, to the operations of commerce, or such things as may in any way contribute to augment the power of the Order. They will transmit all plans of that nature to the Provincial. Should it be a case requiring expedition, he will give him advice of it by some other channel than the Quibus Licets, which the Provincial has not the power of opening."

"XIV. They will follow the same line of conduct with respect to every thing that tends to influence the Order in general; and find means of putting its united forces in motion at one and the same time."

"XV. When an author sets forth principles true in themselves, but which do not as yet suit our general plan of education for the world; or principles the publication of which is premature; every effort must be made to gain over the author; but should all our attempts fail, and we should be unable to entice him into the Order, let him be discredited by every possible means."

"XVI. If a Regent should conceive hopes of succeeding in suppressing any religious houses, and of applying their revenues to our object, for example, to the establishment of proper country schools; he may depend on it, that such a project would be particularly grateful to the Superiors.

"XVII. The Regents will also turn their attention toward a solid plan for establishing a fund to support the widows of the brethren.

"XVIII. One of our most important objects must be, to hinder the servile veneration of the people for Princes from being carried too far. All such abject flattery tends only to make those men worse who are already for the most part of very common and weak understandings. You will show an example of the proper conduct to be held in this respect. Shun all familiarity with them; behave to them politely, but without constraint, that they may honour and fear you. Write and speak of them as you would of other men, that they may be made to recollect that they are but men like other people, and that their authority is a thing purely conventional."

"XIX. When there happens to be a man of merit among our adepts but little known by or entirely unknown to the public, no pains are to be spared to acquire celebrity for him. Let our disguised brethren every where sound the trumpet of his praises, and force envy and party spirit to be silent.

"XX. The essay of our principles and of our schools is most easily and most successfully made in small states. The inhabitants of capitals and commercial towns are too corrupt, too much a prey to their passions, and think themselves too much enlightened, to submit to our lessons.

"XXI. It is useful to send visitors from time to time, or to give a Regent that is travelling the commission to visit the meetings, to ask for the minutes, and to call on the brethren in order to examine their papers or journals, and receive their complaints. — These Plenipotentiaries, presenting themselves in the name of the high Superiors, may correct many faults, and boldly suppress abuses which the Prefects had not the courage to reform, though ready to enforce the commands of the visitor.

"XXII. If our Order cannot establish itself in any particular place with all the forms and regular progress of our degrees, some other form may be assumed. Always have the object in view; that is the essential point. No matter what the cloak may be, provided you succeed; a cloak is however always necessary, for in secrecy our strength principally lies."

"XXIII. For this reason we should always conceal ourselves under the name of some other association. The inferior lodges of Freemasonry are the most convenient cloaks for our grand object, because the world is already familiarized with the idea that nothing of importance, or worthy of their attention can spring from Masonry. — The name of a literary society is also a proper mask for our first classes. Under such a mask, should our assemblies be discovered, we may confidently assert, that the reason of our holding secret assemblies was partly to give a greater interest and charm to our pursuits; partly to keep off the crowd, and not to expose ourselves to the bantering and jealousy of others; in short to hide the weakness of an association as yet but in its infancy."

"XXIV. It is of the utmost importance for us to study the constitutions of other secret societies and to govern them. The Regent is even bound, after having obtained leave of his superiors, to gain admittance into those societies, but he must not undertake too many engagements. This is an additional reason why our Order should remain secret.

"XXV. The higher degrees must always be hidden from the lower. A person more willingly receives orders from a stranger than from men in whom he gradually discovers a multitude of defects. By this precaution one may keep the inferiors in a more proper awe; for they naturally pay greater attention to their behaviour when they think themselves surrounded by persons who are observing them; at first, their virtue may be the effect of constraint, but custom will soon make it habitual."

"XXVI. Never lose sight of the military schools, of the academies, printing presses, libraries, cathedral chapters, or any public establishments that can influence education or government. Let our Regents perpetually attend to the various means, and form plans for making us masters of all these establishments."

"XXVII. In general, and independent of their particular employment, the grand object of our Regents must be an habitual and constant application to every thing which can in any way add to the perfection and to the power of our Order, that it may become for future ages the most perfect model of government that can enter the mind of man;"

## Instructions for the Provincial

"I. The Provincial shall make himself perfect master of the whole constitution of the Order. The system of it should be as familiar to him as if he had invented it."

"II. As a guide for all his actions, he shall adopt the whole government and the instructions already laid down for the Regents and Local Superiors, not neglecting a single rule. "

"III. The Provincial shall be chosen by the Regents of his Province, and be confirmed by the National Superior. The high Superiors (the Areopage and General) have the power of deposing him."

"IV. He shall be a native of, or at least be thoroughly acquainted with the province under his inspection."

"V. He shall be engaged as little as possible in public concerns, or in any other enterprize, that he may devote all his time to the Order."

"VI. He shall assume the character of a man retired from the world, and who only seeks rest."

"VII. He shall fix his residence as nearly as possible in the centre of his province, the better to watch over the different districts."

"VIII. On his being named Provincial, he shall leave his former characteristic, and assume that which the high Superiors shall give him. — The same Superiors will send him the impression of the seal he is to bear, and he will wear it engraved on his ring."

"IX. The archives of the province, which the Regents will have taken care to seal up and carry away on the demise of his predecessor, are to be entrusted to him on his nomination."

"X. The Provincial will monthly transmit the general report of his province to the National Inspector immediately over him. As he himself only receives the reports of the Local Superiors a fortnight after the month is up, he will necessarily be always a month behind-hand, making, for example, the report of May about the end of June, and so on. This report will be subdivided into as many parts as he has Prefects under his inspection. He will carefully note every thing of consequence that has happened in any of the schools or lodges: also the names, ages, country, station in life, and the date of the reversal letters, of each new adept; the high Superiors wishing to have no further information concerning the new adepts until they come to the class of Regent, unless on some particular occasion."

"XI. Beside this monthly report, he is to apply to the National Superior in all extraordinary cases which are not left to his decision. He is also to send in his personal tablets every three months; and he will undertake no political enterprize without having first consulted."

"XII. He has nothing to do with the other Provincials. Let things go on well or ill in a neighbouring province, it is no business of his. If he wishes to ask any thing of the other Provincials, let him apply to the National Inspector."

"XIII. If he has any complaint to make against the Inspector, he will direct his letter Soli or Primo."

"XIV. All the Regents of the province are his counsellors; they are to second and help him in all his enterprizes. If it be convenient to him, he should have two of them near his person to serve him as secretaries."

"XV. He confirms the nominations of all the Superiors of the inferior degrees. He also names the Prefects, but they must be approved by the Director, who can refuse his sanction."

"XVI. He has a right to send the brethren who are pensioned by the Order, and to employ them in those parts of the province where he may think them most useful."

"XVII and XVIII. He transmits the characteristics of the brethren and geographical names of the lodges to the Prefects, as he receives them from the high Superiors."

"XIX. He is also to send the names of the excluded brethren, that an exact list may be preserved in all the assemblies."

"XX. When he has any reprimand to make to a Brother, whom it may be dangerous to offend, he will assume an unknown hand, and the signature of Basyle. This name, which no member of the Order bears, is peculiarly preserved for that object.

"XXI. He will sometimes write to the Inferior degrees; and on the proposition of the Epopts he will decide what books are to be put into the hands of the young adepts according to the degrees they are in. — He is as much as possible to promote libraries, cabinets of natural philosophy, Musæums, collections of manuscripts, &c. in the most convenient parts of his Province; these, it may easily be conceived, are only intended for the adepts.

"XXII. The Provincial opens the letters of the Minor and Major Illuminees which are directed Soli. He also reads the Quibus Licets of the Epopts and Primos of the

Novices; but can neither open the Primo of the Minerval, the Soli of the Knight, nor the Quibus Licet of the Regent.

"XXIII. He shall raise no Brother to the degree of Regent, without having first obtained the consent of the National Inspector.

"XXIV. He is to inform the Dean of the branch of science which each new adept has made choice of on his admission into the Minerval Academy.

"XXV. Lest any of the Archives should be mislaid, he will take care to form but one bundle of all the tablets, reversal letters, and other documents relating to the same adept.

"XXVI. He will apply himself to procure as many co-operators as possible for the Order, in the scientific branches.

"XXVII. He will transmit to the Deans all remarkable treatises or discourses, and every thing relative to the degree of Epopt; for example, the lives historical or characteristic, dissertations, &c.

"XXVIII. If among the Epopts any men be found endowed with great talents, but little fitted for the political government of the Order, the Provincial must devise means of removing them from such functions.

"XXIX. When the Chapters of the Scotch Knights are composed of more than twelve Knights, he will raise the ablest among them to the degree of Epopt.

"XXX. In each Chapter he will have a confidential Epopt, who will be his secret censor or spy.

"XXXI. The Provincial will receive his letters patent from the National Superior—When he issues those for the Chapters of the Scotch Knights, he will make use of the following formula: 'We of the Grand Lodge of the Germanic Orient, constituted Provincial and Master of the district of N N, make known that by these presents we give to the venerable Brother (here is the characteristic and true name of the new Venerable or Master) full powers to erect a secret Chapter of the most holy Scotch Masonry, and to propagate this Royal Art conformably to his instructions by the establishment of new Masonic Lodges of the three symbolic degrees— Given at the Directory of the District—

(L. S.)
Secret Provincial
of the Directory.
without any further signature.

"XXXII. To say every thing in a few words, the Provincial has the special charge of putting his province in a proper situation for attempting every thing for the general good, and for preventing all evil.—Happy the state where our Order shall have acquired such power! Nor will it prove a difficult task for the Provincial who shall implicitly follow the instructions of his high Superiors.—Seconded by so many able men deeply versed in moral sciences, submissive and secretly labouring like himself, there can be no noble enterprize which he may not undertake, nor evil design which he cannot avert—Therefore let there be no connivance at faults; no Nepotism, no private piques; no views but for the general good; no object, no motives but those of the Order. And let the Brethren rely upon us, that we shall never create any Provincials but such as are capable of fulfilling these duties; but let it be also remembered, that we reserve in our hands all the means necessary for chastising the man who should presume to abuse the power he has received from us.

"XXXIII. This power must never be employed but for the good of the Brethren. We should indeed help all whom we can help; but when the circumstances are similar, the members of our society are always to have the preference. — Particularly as to those whose fidelity is proof against all the powers of seduction. In their support let us be prodigal of our toils, our money, our honour, our goods, even our blood; and let the least affront offered to any Illuminee be the general cause of the Order."

# Please Visit the Newly Expanded "Products" Page at

*www.newhermetics.com*
or
*http://shop.vendio.com/centerofchanges/*

to find everything you need for practical New Hermetics magick:

- Magick Mirrors and Crystal Balls
- Ritual Candles
- New Hermetics Incense Blends
- Incense Burners, Candleholders etc.
- Tarot Decks
- Pendulums
- Statuary
- Enochian Temple Equipment
- Light & Sound Mind Machines
- Metaphysical Hypnosis CDs
- Posters and more!

## THE SPIRIT AND THE SWORD
## John Michael Greer

Martial arts are not a distinctly Eastern phenomenon. The West has had numerous fighting forms that have developed sufficiently to be considered Martial arts. However, the vast majority of these Martial disciplines have not survived the advancement of the West toward technological combat. In this fascinating and highly instructive volume, John Michael Greer reveals a little known living tradition of swordsmanship that has survived into the twenty-first century behind the sealed doors of small and secretive fraternal lodges.

Greer integrates these techniques of the sword with the development of the whole person along Qabalistic evolutionary principles that will be familiar to many Western esotericists. What emerges is a highly important component of the Western secret tradition, the nearly lost Art of the Sword.

If you have ever longed to feel the power of live steel in your hand, face to face with a worthy adversary on the field of honorable combat, then this is the book for you.

250 pages                                                                $24.95

## THE BROTHERHOOD OF LIGHT AND DARKNESS
### a novel by Jason Augustus Newcomb

Alexander Sebastian is an armchair occult enthusiast who lacks much direction in life, but his world is turned upside down when his police detective brother-in-law asks him to help identify some magical symbols scrawled at a gruesome, ritualistic homicide. The crime is so horrific that it almost seems the killer might be some sort of demonic creature.

Alex quickly becomes obsessed with the crime, wondering who could be practicing black magick right in his hometown of Arlington, Massachusetts. He decides to find out and is quickly drawn into the underground modern magick scene. He encounters a vast array of odd characters- an obese, narcissistic, drug-peddling adept, a beautiful, coke-snorting, sex magick dominatrix, an insanely jealous Freemason who pontificates with a lisp, and many others. But is one of them a killer? Or is one of them a demonic conjurer?

To find out more, Alex joins the A∴R∴T∴, an international magical fraternity with a sinister reputation, discovering that the murder victim was a member of this group. He soon begins to have unusually vivid and peculiar dreams, and terrifying encounters with what appears to be the world of the supernatural. He can't tell whether these experiences are magical attacks from the killer, or just the product of his overactive imagination. As he tries to separate fact from fiction, and find out who is responsible for murder, Alex also discovers the beginning of his personal spiritual journey into the world of magical awakening.

This story is drawn largely from Newcomb's own personal experiences over the past twenty years actively participating in the modern magical community. It comes out of his real life encounters with secret magical fraternities and the unique, eccentric people that populate this sub-culture. Fans of Harry Potter or the DaVinci Code will discover what the world of magick and secret societies really looks like when you're personally involved. It reveals the world of the unknown as it truly exists, with an insider's view of the real world of Witches, Wizards, Rosicrucians and magical creatures.

308 pages, Hardcover                                                    $39.95

## NEW HERMETICS EQUINOX JOURNAL VOLUME 1
### edited by Jason Augustus Newcomb

This first volume of the New Hermetics Equinox Journal includes numerous updates and advancements in the New Hermetics techniques and ideas, a comparative record of several New Hermeticists conducting the "Tarot Archetype Pathworking" technique with the twenty-two trumps along with some helpful hints for students interested in greater success with this practice. This volume also includes an article on the eight seasonal holiday festivals from a New Hermetics perspective, and a collection of poetry inspired by the New Hermetics.

220 pages $21.95

The New
Hermetics
Equinox
Journal

Volume Two

edited by Jason Augustus Newcomb

NEW HERMETICS EQUINOX JOURNAL VOLUME 2
edited by Jason Augustus Newcomb
    The second volume of the New Hermetics Equinox Journal contains sev-
eral practical articles by Jason Augustus Newcomb on Angelic Vision Magick,
Crystal Balls and Magick Mirrors, Creating Inner Harmony within the New
Hermetics and the function and role of the imagination in magical practice.
This volume also has a wonderful article from Philip H. Farber on creating a
personal pantheon of gods as well as an extensive interview with psychedelic
DMT research doctor Rick Strassman MD. Additionally, this book contains
other great practical articles ranging from Alchemy to the Eight Sabbats or
seasonal festivals.
**200 pages**                                                         **$21.95**


VOLUMES FOUR, FIVE, SIX AND SO ON
COMING AT EACH EQUINOX!

## PRACTICAL ENOCHIAN MAGICK
### Jason Augustus Newcomb

Enochian Magick is arguably the most intriguing and potent form of ceremonial magick available today. Dr. John Dee, a prominent philosopher in the Elizabethan court, literally received this system of magick from angels through the scrying mediumship of Edward Kelly. Practical Enochian Magick offers a complete approach to conducting the magical system of Dr. John Dee for the modern adept. Instructions in the practical use of all three major parts of the Enochian system are contained in these pages: the Four Watchtowers, the Thirty Aethyrs and the Heptarchia Mystica. Rather than a mere rehash of Golden Dawn material this book offers an approach that honors both the innovations of the Golden Dawn and the essence of the original Dee materials in an un-dogmatic and nonsectarian format that will be extremely accessible to the New Hermetics Adept. Although this book is particularly designed for students of the New Hermetics, anyone interested in actually making use of Enochian Magick as a practicing occultist will find this book incredibly useful.

328 pages                                                                                    $26.95

## ENOCHIAN MAGICK TOOLBOOK
### Jason Augustus Newcomb

This companion volume to Practical Enochian Magick is a large format 8.5"
X 11" full color book designed to help you get started conducting the rituals
of Enochian Magick quickly and easily. This book contains full color prints of
the four watchtowers, all of the rituals and temple openings as well as the
Enochian keys on parchment scripts for use in your rituals, the talismans of
the Heptarchia Mystica and other ritual accouterments to help you get started
with this system of magick immediately.
132 pages                                                    $55.95

www.ingramcontent.com/pod-product-compliance
Lightning Source LLC
Chambersburg PA
CBHW030531030726
47495CB00004B/951